Authentic Adventism

William G. Johnsson

Authentic Adventism

William G. Johnsson

OAK & ACORN
PUBLISHING
Westlake Village, California

For information contact:
Oak & Acorn Publishing
PO Box 5005
Westlake Village, CA 91359-5005

Cover design: Lauren Smith and Oak & Acorn

First Edition: September 2018

10 9 8 7 6 5 4 3 2 1

For Steve
colleague and friend
authentic Adventist

Contents

Preface xi

PART I:
Introduction

Chapter 1
Barley Greens and Beards—Who Decides? 3

PART II:
Marks of Authentic Adventism

Chapter 2
The Elephant in the Room 11

Chapter 3
Church Without Walls 25

Chapter 4
Heart Religion 41

Chapter 5
Transparent as Light 57

Chapter 6
Present Truth 73

Chapter 7
The Other Elephant 89

Chapter 8
The Call of the Kingdom 105

Chapter 9
His Love, Our Love 121

PART III:
Coda

Chapter 10
Two Women, Two Seats 139

The Last Word 151

Preface

I left my roses to write this book.

I didn't plan to write it. I didn't want to write it. Another book means stepping back into a surreal existence punctuated by night vigils, exhilarating new ideas, and tough, grinding work. And, when it's done, angry saints.

But the Voice said: "Another book." And before I'd written a word, the Voice gave me the title: "Authentic Adventism."

It's a follow-up to *Where Are We Headed? Adventism after San Antonio*. That book has enjoyed an enthusiastic reception to a degree that amazes me. I guess it works because of its timeliness: it gives voice to what a lot of pastors and others are thinking but are too afraid to speak openly.

But I have a rose garden. Yes, I have a rose garden. Small, but beautiful. Noelene and I lived in the Washington, DC, area for 34 years. I tried to grow roses, but it was war—fungus, black-leaf, Japanese beetles. To produce a pretty rose you had to subject life and limb to foul-smelling, toxic sprays.

Now we live in Southern California, where it doesn't rain and the sun shines every day. No need to spray. No beetle traps. My roses bloom big, abundant, beautiful.

I love my rose garden. The rose garden is safe, tranquil.

But the Voice said: "Another book." After *Where Are We Headed?*

hit the fan in the Spring of 2017, a few people said, "Great! Now you should do a follow-up." To which I replied, "No, thank you. That's for someone else to handle."

But the Voice. I came in from the rose garden and went to work.

"Authentic" Adventism suggests that there's an inauthentic Adventism. Could that be the case?

Yes. Unfortunately, sadly, yes.

Too much talk without the walk.

Too many platitudes.

Too much patting ourselves on the back.

Too many clichés.

Too much fear.

Too much show.

Too much pretense.

Too much "us" and "them"-ing.

Too many racial slurs and innuendos.

Too much playing religious games.

Too much concern about what others will say.

Too much concern to look right and sound right.

Too much religious baloney.

My message in this book to the church I love is: "GET REAL!"

Inauthentic Adventism—the millennials smell it a mile off and head for the door.

We have a problem, a huge problem. We baptize thousands of converts, but we can't hold our own youth. Could it be that it's because they see us as phony?

Hence, another book to follow *Where Are We Headed?* It's a heart book, not a series of carefully researched essays. It's my heart cry over what I see and hear in the Adventist family.

I don't have all the answers, but I have convictions. I will try to share them honestly, openly, candidly. I want to make myself vulnerable.

Why? Because I'm a dreamer, an idealist.

I dream of authentic Adventism:

I dream of a church without hate,

I dream of a church without walls,

I dream of a church without phoniness,

I dream of a church without cover-ups,

I dream of a church without boasting,

I dream of a church without fear,

I dream of a church without discrimination,

I dream of a church that is open to advancing truth,

I dream of a church that gets its hands dirty,

I dream of a church where love reigns,

I dream of a church where Jesus is All.

As I worked on the manuscript, I rode a wave of enthusiastic support from many people. In particular: from Dr. Robert Soderblom, Dr. Shandelle Henson, Dr. Priscilla Costa, and Dr. Johnny Thomas. Members of Adventist congregations in Portland, OR; Boulder, CO; and Seattle, WA, came out on Sabbath afternoons to offer suggestions for content. Others in England and Australia sent ideas online. Ray Tetz again coordinated all aspects of the book production; he was ably assisted by Rosy Tetz, who edited the manuscript, and by Alberto Valenzuela, who handled lay-out and design. My heartfelt thanks to all. In addition, my appreciation to Matthew Korpman for granting permission to reproduce his paper given at the Adventist Society of Religious Studies in November 2017 and printed in *Spectrum* magazine.

As always in my writing, thanks to the Lord and then to the one who keys my scrawl into the computer. To my best friend, counselor, unfailing source of encouragement—Noelene.

PART I

Introduction

"This above all:
to thine own self be true,
And it must follow, as night the day,
Thou canst not then be false to any man."
—William Shakespeare

CHAPTER ONE

Barley Greens and Beards —Who Decides?

Who decides who is an authentic Adventist?

His eyes glowed with the fire of a true believer. Seizing my arm, he proclaimed dramatically: "This is what the biggest animals to ever live on this earth ate. This is what the biggest animals today eat—grass!"

I was browsing among the rows of shelves packed with vitamins, supplements, minerals, and herbs. It was an amazing, dazzling display of pills and potions—everything one could need, want, or imagine for health and longevity.

My reverie was interrupted by a tall man with white hair and blazing eyes, presumably an employee of the store. Quickly sizing me up—correctly—as someone new to the display, he launched into a cross-examination.

"What did you eat for breakfast yesterday?"

"What did you eat for dinner?"

"What did you eat for supper?"

Almost every food I listed brought forth the rejoinder: "No energy in that!"

And then: "Listen, I'll show you how to get lots of energy in your diet." And so to the aisle where the high-potency, big animal, grass products were stocked.

He took a huge can from the shelf and pointed to its contents: barley grass, wheatgrass, green kamut, alfalfa grass, spirulina, chlorella. The dinosaurs would have loved it.

He left the large can in my hands and went off in search of another victim. Shocked by the price, I quickly replaced the can on the shelf. But the guy had been so intense, so earnest—and what was there for me to lose? I found the product in a much smaller edition and headed for the cashier.

My friends, I have to tell you that I was intrigued by what was inside the can. Slicing through the tinfoil top that safeguarded its secrets, I found what looked for all the world like lawn seed. The faint, fresh odor of newly cut grass wafted out.

The next morning I decided to try it on oatmeal. Adding a modest helping of cut grass (I am a modest person), I sat down with a sense of adventure. This was the food eaten by the biggest animals that ever lived on the planet! This is the diet of the largest animals that still live in our world!

Somehow that recommendation didn't seem as impressive as when it came from the lips of the true believer. Did I want to be among the elephants, mammoths, and hippos?

No way.

On the cooked oatmeal the grass took on a greenish-yellow hue. I needed dark glasses for this breakfast.

And it tasted like…what? Like grass, of course.

Did it give me the energy boost that the true believer promised? Maybe—who knows? I never returned to the experiment. The can of grass still sits in the kitchen. I'll gladly mail to anyone who's longing for it.

Now, I must quickly add that I mean no disrespect for anyone who eats barley greens or any other particular item that they find useful for their health. More power to you, friend; be assured that I'm not mocking you.

My point is simply this: for some Adventists a particular item of diet takes on critical importance. They can't imagine authentic Adventism not including barley greens, or whatever.

So who decides?

Then there are beards. Did you know that way back the General Conference Committee mandated that all ministers be bearded? It was the custom of the times. That's why when you look at photographs of the pioneers you see a bunch of men with a lot of hair on their physiognomy, looking very serious. (And that was because in the early days of photography, you had to hold yourself without moving for a long time. Too long to keep a smile.)

Beards then, but that test of the true Adventist gradually faded—although I was informed that the beard requirement has never been expunged from the books.

Funnily, when I taught at the Seminary at Andrews University, the rule for students was—guess what? No beards permitted!

Barley greens, beards: will the authentic Adventist please stand up?

Is it anything goes, then? I'll have my list of authentic Adventism and you have yours?

No, not at all. Stay with me.

Well, maybe you say, the answer is the 28 Fundamental Beliefs. That's where you find the real McCoy—anyone who accepts all 28 and puts them into practice.

That's a good answer. Doctrine is important. A person has to keep the seventh-day Sabbath to be a Seventh-day Adventist.

But is getting our doctrines straight all there is? Listen to what God said anciently to His people:

> Quit your worship charades.
> I can't stand your trivial religious games:
> Monthly conferences, weekly Sabbaths, special meetings—
>   meetings, meetings, meetings—I can't stand one more!
> Meetings for this, meetings for that. I hate them!
>   You've worn me out!
> I'm sick of your religion, religion, religion,
>   while you go right on sinning.
> When you put on your next prayer-performance,
>   I'll be looking the other way.
> No matter how long or loud or often you pray,
>   I'll not be listening.
> And do you know why? Because you've been tearing
>   people to pieces, and your hands are bloody.
> Go home and wash up.
>   Clean up your act.
> Sweep your lives clean of your evildoings
>   so I don't have to look at them any longer.

Say no to wrong.
　　Learn to do good.
Work for justice.
　　Help the down-and-out.
Stand up for the homeless.
　　Go to bat for the defenseless (Isaiah 1:13-17).

Here are people who look like they're doing right—honoring the Sabbath, following all the religious duties. But God is not pleased with them. There is something more that they lacked.

Fast forward to 2018. Consider with me a couple of case studies.

Here's an Adventist who scores 100 percent on the Fundamental Beliefs but who tells jokes disparaging an ethnic group that is different from his.

Authentic Adventist?

She cringes at those jokes but does not speak out.

Authentic Adventist?

He's a church elder but hates Muslims. He says he'd like to see America "nuke" them all.

Authentic Adventist?

At church everyone holds him in high regard; he's a model Adventist. At home his wife and kids live with a different picture: he's a demanding, harsh bully.

Authentic Adventist?

I don't think so—not in any of the cases above.

If authentic Adventism goes beyond what we believe, what is it? And who gets to decide?

Jesus.

He and He alone shows us what authentic Adventism really is.

Not just what it believes—how it *acts*, how it lives.

So here's my approach in this book: Every quality that you think designates authentic Adventism has to pass the Jesus test. You have to first find it—find it clearly and unequivocally, not by fudging, inference, or slight of hand—in the life and teachings of Jesus.

If you can't find it in the Gospels, it fails the Jesus test.

The chapters that follow set out a series of life qualities that I believe define authentic Adventism. To make the point, I commence each chapter with a story about Jesus or a teaching passage from the Gospels.

This is my attempt to demonstrate authentic Adventism. I don't suggest that my criteria exhaust the topic. You, perhaps, will want to suggest additional ideas.

You may add, but not subtract. What I suggest here is a minimalist list. Authentic Adventism cannot be less than this list because Jesus is the gold standard.

It may be more, but never less.

This book is all about Jesus.

What He is like.

What we will be like if we are true followers of Jesus.

Authentic.

So climb aboard. Fasten your seatbelt. Get ready for the ride of your life.

PART II

Marks of Authentic Adventism

"Authenticity starts in the heart."
—Brian D'Angelo

CHAPTER TWO

The Elephant in the Room

Leaving that place, Jesus withdrew to the region of Tyre and Sidon. A Canaanite woman from that vicinity came to him, crying out, "Lord, Son of David, have mercy on me! My daughter is demon-possessed and suffering terribly."

Jesus did not answer a word. So his disciples came to him and urged him, "Send her away, for she keeps crying out after us."

He answered, "I was sent only to the lost sheep of Israel."

The woman came and knelt before him. "Lord, help me!" she said.

He replied, "It is not right to take the children's bread and toss it to the dogs."

"Yes it is, Lord," she said. "Even the dogs eat the crumbs that fall from their master's table."

Then Jesus said to her, "Woman, you have great faith! Your request is granted." And her daughter was healed at that moment (Matthew 15:21-28, NIV).

W arning: The content of this chapter may make you un-comfortable. It makes me uncomfortable.

We don't want to talk about this topic, especially in the United States. Over the years I have observed a phenomenon that puzzled me for a long time: Whenever I mentioned this area in a sermon, the audience, who had been following my remarks, put their heads down.

What is going on? I wondered.

Eventually it hit me—the topic made the hearers uncomfortable. They didn't want to hear about it, wished that I would leave it and go on to something else.

Without realizing it, I had pointed to the elephant in the room.

What is the elephant in the room? Race relations.

It's time for us, especially Seventh-day Adventists, to be honest. Time to be open. Time to talk about what we, by common consent, avoid—except for off-the-record conversations with trusted friends.

For authentic Adventism, there can be no elephants in the room. Even if most men and women in the society around us turn away, we cannot. We are followers of Jesus of Nazareth, who instructed us: "The eye is the lamp of the body. So, if your eye is healthy, your whole body will be full of light; but if your eye is unhealthy, your whole body will be full of darkness" (Matthew 6:22-23, NRSV).

How important is this matter? We could go back a long, long way in American history, but let's begin with a horrific 24-hour period in Charlottesville, Virginia.

Charlottesville, Virginia

August 12, 2017: An uneasy hush lies over the quiet college town where Thomas Jefferson founded the University of Virginia. All week rumors have circulated about a big rally of white nationalists. They plan to gather in Emancipation Park to protest against the removal of the statue of Robert E. Lee.

Throughout the day vehicles arrive from all around the United States. They bring hundreds of white nationalists, white supremacists, neo-Confederates, Ku Klux Klansmen, neo–Nazis, militia groups, and others. Some carry semi-automatic weapons and shields. Banners spit out hate, racial rage, anti-Semitism.

Friday night a column of about 250 people, mainly young white males, begins to form. They prepare to march in a procession of flaming torches reminiscent of the Hitler Youth marches of Nazi Germany. As they march they yell: "Blood and soil!" "You will not replace us!" "Jews will not replace us!"

They are met by a group of counterprotesters. Soon there is chaos. Shoves, punches, chemical irritants, taunts, insults, obscenities, injuries.

The next day is worse. Rallygoers arrive in contingents, carrying nationalist banners and chanting slogans. Many carry shields, clubs, pistols, long guns. They bring with them swastikas, Confederate flags, anti-Semitic and anti-Muslim banners. Many carry sticks and signs. They are opposed by church groups, civil rights leaders, and onlookers.

Most stores and restaurants close for the day.

Then another force arrives: a militia group dressed in full camouflage and armed with semi-automatic rifles and pistols.

The two sides scream at each other. Mayhem explodes. Each side swings sticks, throws punches, sprays chemicals. Bottles and rocks fly back and forth.

At last the authorities intervene: the disturbance is declared an unlawful assembly. The crowd is ordered to disperse.

As the right-wing groups begin to leave, they continue to exchange taunts and insults with the counterprotesters. "Go back to Africa," one yells to a black woman. Another screams: "Dylann Roof was a hero!" referring to the white supremacist who killed nine African Americans in a church in Charleston, South Carolina.

The long, tragic day appears to be over. But it isn't.

Around 1 p.m., a rallygoer roars his Dodge Challenger at a crowd of pedestrians. The car plows into one group, then reverses into another.

One woman is killed. Nineteen others are injured.

But the end is not yet. That evening a state police helicopter monitoring the rally crashes. Two state troopers die in the crash.

Tally for the day: three dead, 19 injured.

The images of hate, racial rage, violence, and death fly across the nation and around the world.

A day of shame.

A deeply disturbing day.

After Charlottesville

I'm no expert, but I think we have entered a dark, unpredictable phase in the United States. How it will turn out is uncertain. But of this I'm totally convinced: *It's time to wake up and speak out!*

Noelene and I were born and raised in Australia. It's a wonderful country, and we loved it.

Forty-two years ago we came to the United States to work. The Adventist Church invited us to join the faculty of the Seminary at Andrew University. We were there five years, then we went to Washington, DC.

We fell in love with America, but we felt strong ties to our native land. We were here more than 20 years before we took out papers to become United States citizens. If we have to pay taxes, we want a say in what's happening—we wanted to be able to vote!

Forty-two years—I'm still trying to figure out America. America, my country. We've lived in Nashville, TN, in Berrien Springs, MI, in Silver Spring, MD, in Loma Linda, CA—north, south, east, west.

America the beautiful—a country so blessed, so beautiful. It's amazing. It's wonderful.

Look at California: a thousand miles of coast, snow-capped mountains, redwood forests, deserts that burst into color when the rains come back. And Yosemite—oh Yosemite! Nothing like it, nothing close to like it anywhere else on earth.

But in this land of purple mountain's majesty and amber waves of grain, nature at times shows a dark side:

Here in California, the ground moves under our feet. We talk about the Big One. Not "if," but "when."

In America's heartland, so bountiful in natural endowments, tornadoes swoop down without warning and level everything in their path.

In the East, storm centers form in the Atlantic, gathering moisture and power as they roll west. Becoming hurricanes, they roar with fury as they pound Florida and the Eastern Seaboard.

The dark side of America.

And the culture tends to mirror nature.

On one hand, America is a land of unparalleled opportunity—a country where, if you can produce the goods, the doors open wide to you (especially if your skin is the right color).

Americans are incredibly generous. They enjoy life—especially in California! They like humor; they smile easily and more often than people anywhere else in the world.

But—there's a dark side.

America is the land of the Ku Klux Klan, of lynching, of terrible injustice and cruelty.

Slavery has cursed this land.

It cursed the black man.

It cursed the white man.

The curse continues.

It messes up relationships. It divides us. It makes us suspicious. It makes us afraid.

I am white. I don't think I can ever understand what it's like to be black. I've never had to be concerned that a police officer will pull me over and ask to see proof that the car I'm driving really belongs to me. I've never had to instruct my son to be ultra careful if a cop pulls him over because of a broken tail light, because I wanted him to come home alive.

The numbers are staggering:

The United States has 4.5 percent of the world's population, but it houses 22 percent of the world's prison population—currently, more than 2.2 million. African Americans are incarcerated at five times the rate of whites. (If you're black, you have more than five times the likelihood of spending time in prison.)

The dark side of America!

After Barak Obama was elected president, a lot of people said: "This proves that racism is dead in America."

Were they ever wrong! Racism was very much alive. Obama's election tore off the Band-Aid. Many were angry that a black person was president. They tried to prove he wasn't really born an American.

They refused to respect him. They set out to cause him to fail.

Militia groups sprang up by the hundreds. They spewed out hate. They armed themselves with heavy weapons. They talked about making America great again—meaning making America white again.

And then came Charlottesville.

You saw the images on TV. I did and could hardly believe my eyes.

Hundreds of white men marching, armed, holding flaming torches.

Swastikas, the flag of the Nazis. And chanting, "Blood and soil!"— the Nazi hate cry.

Listen, we fought a war to save the world from Nazi Germany. More than 400,000 Americans gave their lives to keep them from taking over.

That Friday night in Charlottesville, Jews were meeting in a synagogue for Sabbath services. A mob carrying Nazi flags and shouting hate slogans blocked the entrance. The congregants were afraid; they locked the doors.

The service ended, but the mob was still outside. The worshipers had to stay put for another hour. At last they slipped out the back door.

Is this the United States?

Are we in America or in Nazi Germany of the 1930s?

The Tiergarten

The images from Charlottesville remind me of a book I read a few years ago: *In the Garden of Beasts* by Erik Larson.

The book brings to life the years 1933-1939. It's about the American ambassador to Germany, William Dodd. Hitler had just come to power. Chapter by chapter you see the Nazis taking over the country. You see big parades and "Heil Hitler" salutes. Thugs work the crowds, beating up anyone who fails to salute.

I found the book bone chilling, but that all happened years ago. It could never happen here.

And then I saw the images from Charlottesville.

The German state-sponsored persecution led to the death of:

6 million Jews,

250,000 people with disabilities,

thousands of the LGBT community,

200,000 gypsies.

This is what Nazism meant! Why would today's young people want to identify with them? Did you notice the age of the guy who drove his vehicle into the crowd, injuring 19 and killing Heather Heyer, age 32, a legal assistant?

He was only 20.

It seems a wave of hate is spreading over America. Can *anything* be done about it? *Can we do something to stop the hate?*

I say Yes! But only in Jesus of Nazareth. Government can make laws—and I am all for just laws—but only Jesus can change attitudes, can root out the ugliness that we harbor in our hearts.

An Intriguing Story

Let's turn to an intriguing story in the Gospels. It's sort of shocking, but that's Jesus all the way. He shocks us. He upsets us. He isn't the "meek and mild" fellow who makes you feel comfortable. No, He's shocking. He's radical. He upsets the tables and chairs in the Temple. He will upset your life, if you let Him.

You can find this story in Matthew 15:21-28. I put it at the beginning of this chapter, to set the tone. Turn back and refresh your memory.

I call her The Woman Who Wouldn't Go Away. She keeps on trying, keeps working on Jesus. She's sure that only Jesus can give her the help that she needs for her daughter. I love this woman who loves her daughter so much that she refuses to be deterred.

Note: She's not Jewish. Jesus has left Galilee and is over by the Mediterranean coast. The woman is a foreigner, a Canaanite.

Jesus surely acts strangely. The woman is shouting to Him, but He doesn't say a word.

At last the disciples have had enough. "Send her away," they urge Jesus. "Stop her shouting!"

Then Jesus speaks.

To the disciples He says: "I was sent only to help people from Israel."

She's a Gentile. Only Jews qualify for God's favors.

But the woman refuses to quit. Now she comes and kneels at Jesus' feet. She implores Him. "Lord, help me."

Then Jesus says something really harsh. "It's not fair to take the food meant for the children and throw it to the dogs."

Ouch! Dogs!

He's calling her a dog?

What's going on? Can this be Jesus?

But even with this massive put-down the woman doesn't give up. She flashes back a brilliant answer: "Yes, Lord, yet even the dogs eat the crumbs that fall from their master's table!"

I marvel at this woman—this woman who won't go away. Three snubs from Jesus, and she still keeps trying:

First, He says nothing. He ignores her. He gives her the silent treatment. That can be worse than a stream of abuse. Some of you have been on the receiving end of the silent treatment. It's like you are suddenly invisible. You know how painful that can feel.

Second, He says that He has come to help only Jews, not Gentiles, so she is out of luck.

Then third, cruelest of all, He calls her a dog. And dogs don't have a place at the table.

How could this foreign woman keep on trying in the face of these three insults?

Well, the story isn't what it seems. The problem is this: when we read the stories of Jesus in the Gospels, we read cold words on paper. We *read*, we don't *hear*.

We don't hear the tone of Jesus' voice.

We don't know the expression on His face.

We don't know if His eyes gave the woman a message different from what His words conveyed.

Jesus must have given her non-verbal messages. Something gave the woman hope to keep on asking. The disciples only heard His words; she saw *how* He spoke.

We do this all the time. To make a point, we'll say just the opposite of what we feel.

I had a friend like that. His name was Wayne McFarland—"Dr. Mac."

We loved each other so much that as soon as we'd meet up we'd start trading insults—hilarious insults. Once we held public meetings together in Aberdeen, Scotland. We were sitting in a restaurant exchanging barbs and laughing our heads off. People at other tables were looking at us and asking the waiter what we were drinking so they could order some.

The Canaanite woman got it. She saw where Jesus was going in the conversation. Did she have a smile on her face as she came back at Jesus' cruel words, calling her a dog? I think maybe she did.

Dogs? OK, then I'll be a dog. Let the children eat at the table. Just let me have a few crumbs that fall under the table. **But please help my daughter!**

Jesus said, smiling now: "Woman, great is your faith! You have your wish."

And her daughter was healed instantly.

The disciples listened to the exchange, but it was essentially a private conversation between Jesus and the woman.

At the end of it all the disciples were shaking their heads and asking one another, "What was *that* all about?"

Well, what was it all about? Jesus was role-playing. He was playing the role of the disciples. To them, this woman was a nuisance. She was annoying them. They just wanted her out of there. And she was, after all, a foreigner.

In their attitude, the disciples were just like the rest of the Jews. Remember the prayer that Jews (men, of course) used to pray each day: "Praised be God that he has not created me a gentile; praised be God that he has not created me a woman; praised be God that he has not created me an ignorant man."

That's the way the disciples had been brought up. That's what Jewish culture had taught them. But Jesus wanted to shake them up. He wanted to help them see themselves as God saw them. That they were heartless, cruel, and arrogant in their attitude to the foreigner.

None of us asked to be born. None of us got to choose who our parents would be or where we would grow up.

We arrived. That's where we are.

Without conscious thought, we take in attitudes and prejudices from the family. From the culture around us.

Does the culture belittle people whose skin is a different color? So do we.

Does the culture slight people whose sexuality is different from the mainstream? So do we.

Is the culture suspicious toward those whose religion is different? So are we.

That's the way for all of us: born into prejudice, hatred, stereotypes.

But we don't have to stay there. We can change. Our eyes can be opened to see ourselves as we are—as God sees us. And as God sees other people, all other people, as His sons and daughters.

I grew up in Australia, and I grew up racist. If you'd told me that, I'd have laughed and said, "My friend, you are dead wrong!" I could point to my friend from Ethiopia, Tshome Wagaw. His skin was very black. During summer vacation from Avondale College, we went door-to-door selling religious books. I struggled; he broke all the sales records. He'd come up to a door, flash his brilliant smile, and say: "Hello, I am Tshoma Wagaw." And the housewives would say, "What are you selling; I want one."

Tshoma stayed at our house. Ate at our table.

Me, racist? Never!

But I was. It took several years for me to realize it.

Noelene and I married straight out of college and went to India as missionaries. We stayed in India 15 years. We loved India; we loved the people.

And slowly, slowly I began to change. Slowly I began to see myself and be ashamed.

I wasn't prejudiced against all people of color. But I was prejudiced toward the Australian Aboriginal people. I grew up looking down on them. Everybody did. We saw them as not quite human.

It took living in India to open my eyes. Or maybe I should say: it was the Lord, working through the Indian environment, who opened my eyes.

The Bottom Line

What is the bottom line after Charlottesville? I'd say five things:

1. Pray for the Lord to open your eyes so that you see yourself as you really are. Let Him shine the spotlight of His love on the ugly crevices of your soul where the demons of hate and bigotry hide.

2. Speak up against hate, anywhere and everywhere. Speak out on social media. Speak out at your workplace. Speak out in your home. Speak out in your school. Speak out in your church. Don't let hate speech get by without calling it out.

3. Root out racial slurs, jokes, innuendos. Occasionally, out of the blue, snatches of a ditty that I sang way, way back come out of the woodwork of my mind. A catchy tune, but blatantly racist. Stories, jokes, epithets—don't give them quarter. Banish them; keep on banishing them.

4. Become a change agent. Spread love instead of hate. Be intentional: Make a friend of someone from a different country. Make a friend of someone who practices a different religion.

5. Ask God to help you surround yourself with an oasis of love. An oasis of caring. An oasis of compassion. The world desperately needs it.

The best tweet to come out of Charlottesville came from Barak Obama. Quoting Nelson Mandela, he said: "No one is born hating another person because of the color of his skin or his background or his religion. People must learn to hate, and if they can learn to hate, they can be taught to love, for love comes more naturally to the human heart than its opposite."

May God open our hearts to love today—and every day.

That is authentic Adventism.

CHAPTER THREE

Church Without Walls

So Jesus left the Judean countryside and went back to Galilee.

To get there, he had to pass through Samaria. He came into Sychar, a Samaritan village that bordered the field Jacob had given his son Joseph. Jacob's well was still there. Jesus, worn out by the trip, sat down at the well. It was noon.

A woman, a Samaritan, came to draw water. Jesus said, "Would you give me a drink of water?" (His disciples had gone to the village to buy food for lunch.)

The Samaritan woman, taken aback, asked, "How come you, a Jew, are asking me, a Samaritan woman, for a drink?" (Jews in those days wouldn't be caught dead talking to Samaritans.)

Jesus answered, "If you knew the generosity of God and who I am, you would be asking me for a drink, and I would give you fresh, living water."

The woman said, "Sir, you don't even have a bucket to draw with, and this well is deep. So how are you going to get this 'living water'? Are you a better man than our ancestor Jacob, who dug this well and drank from it, he and his sons and livestock, and passed it down to us?"

Jesus said, "Everyone who drinks this water will get thirsty again and again. Anyone who drinks the water I give will never thirst—not ever. The water I give will be an artesian spring within, gushing fountains of endless life."

The woman said, "Sir, give me this water so I won't ever get thirsty, won't ever have to come back to this well again!"

He said, "Go call your husband and then come back."

"I have no husband," she said.

"That's nicely put: 'I have no husband.' You've had five husbands, and the man you're living with now isn't even your husband. You spoke the truth there, sure enough."

"Oh, so you're a prophet! Well, tell me this: Our ancestors worshiped God at this mountain, but you Jews insist that Jerusalem is the only place for worship, right?"

"Believe me, woman, the time is coming when you Samaritans will worship the Father neither here at this mountain nor there in Jerusalem. You worship guessing in the dark; we Jews worship in the clear light of day. God's way of salvation is made available through the Jews. But the time is coming—it has, in fact, come—when what you're called will not matter and where you go to worship will not matter.

"It's who you are and the way you live that count before God. Your worship must engage your spirit in the pursuit of truth. That's the kind of people the Father is out looking for: those who are simply and honestly themselves before him in their worship. God is sheer being itself—Spirit. Those who worship him must do it out of their very being, their spirits, their true selves, in adoration."

The woman said, "I don't know about that. I do know that the Messiah is coming. When he arrives, we'll get the whole story."

"I am he," said Jesus. "You don't have to wait any longer or look any further."

Just then his disciples came back. They were shocked. They couldn't believe he was talking with that kind of a woman. No one said what they were all thinking, but their faces showed it.

The woman took the hint and left. In her confusion she left her water pot. Back in the village she told the people, "Come see a man who knew all about the things I did, who knows me inside and out. Do you think this could be the Messiah?" And they went out to see for themselves....

Many of the Samaritans from that village committed themselves to him because of the woman's witness: "He knew all about the things I did. He knows me inside and out!" They asked him to stay on, so Jesus stayed two days. A lot more people entrusted their lives to him when they heard what he had to say. They said to the woman, "We're no longer taking this on your say-so. We've heard it for ourselves and know it for sure. He's the Savior of the world!" (John 4:3-30, 39-42).

Jesus wasn't your average Seventh-day Adventist.

I'm glad He wasn't. If Jesus were your average Seventh-day Adventist, this story wouldn't have happened.

Here He is, sitting by a well in the middle of the day. It's hot, and He's tired and hungry. He and His disciples have walked all morning. They're on the way from Judea in the south to Galilee in the north—a hike of some 90 miles.

They find this well and break their journey. Jesus sits down in the shade of a tree while the others go looking for a village where they can buy some food.

If Jesus were your average Seventh-day Adventist, they wouldn't be here. The people in these parts aren't *nice* folks. They don't like Jews and the feeling is mutual. When Jews go back and forth between the south and the north, they avoid this territory. Instead of traveling in a straight line, they detour to the east and follow the road up the Jordan valley. The Jordan route, though longer, skirts Samaria. But this day Jesus has done what the average Jew would not do. He has led His disciples slap-bang into hostile country.

A woman comes to the well with her water pot. In this society, as in many others, women's work means carrying the water for the needs of the household. It's hard work—water is heavy, and the water pot is big. The women come to the well in the morning or the evening when the burning sun doesn't add to the burden of the work. They gather by the well and exchange gossip and pleasantries before lifting the water pots to their heads.

But this woman has long since tired of the accusing eyes and biting tongues of the women. This woman is a bad woman: she wears not just one A but A's all over her shawl.

She comes to the well at midday as she always does and—*oh no! There's someone here! It's a man—and he's one of those stinking Jews.*

Without her speaking a word, Jesus can feel the animosity radiating from her person. She wishes that He weren't there. He's intruded on her space.

What are the odds that Jesus and this woman will even talk? That the ice will crack and that they will develop a long and searching exchange?

Zero.

If Jesus were your average Seventh-day Adventist.

But He isn't, and it happens.

Four walls divide Jesus from the woman. Each of them is solid, dug deep in centuries of tradition and folklore.

Wall #1: She's a woman. Jesus is a rabbi, a religious teacher, and rabbis don't talk with women. Rabbis know that women are dangerous, that they can turn a man from the straight and narrow with their bewitching eyes. Some rabbis, when they see women approaching them on the street, avert their gaze and walk straight ahead—sometimes into a wall or an ox-cart! Better to get black and blue than to be ensnared by a woman.

If Jesus were your average rabbi (read SDA), He would have prayed like the other rabbis: "Blessed are You, Lord God of the universe, who did not make me a woman."

But Jesus isn't your average rabbi. Rabbis went around from town to town, village to village, accompanied by disciples who hung on their every word. They were rabbis in training. And all of them—always—were male.

Not so with Jesus, however. His entourage includes women, a lot of them. Luke names several and says that there were "many" more (Luke 8:1-3).

Some of them had been cured by Jesus. One of them, Mary of Magdala, had been demon-possessed before Jesus set her free. Some of these women had husbands who occupied important positions in society, like Joanna, wife of Chuza, who managed the household affairs of Herod Antipas, ruler over Galilee and Perea.

These women were independently wealthy, and out of their resources they bankrolled the itinerant ministry of Jesus.

Jesus' actions must have been regarded as highly questionable, utterly inappropriate for a rabbi. Tongues wagged. Religious leaders tut-tutted. Shocking!

So it's not so surprising to find Jesus taking the initiative with the woman who comes to draw water. Except that it is. She isn't a genteel lady like Susanna, Joanna, and others in Jesus' disciple party. No, no, anything but.

Wall #2: She's a Samaritan. The Samaritans were a mongrel people. Their history went back some 500 years to the days when Israel had its own kings. The 10 northern tribes had broken away from the south after Solomon died, and they set up their own kingdom with Samaria as its capital. Eventually, however, they were overrun by the Assyrian armies under Sargon.

Among the nations of antiquity, the Assyrians were a byword for cruelty. One of their diabolical practices involved chaining captives with large fishhooks through their jaws. To ensure that captured peoples wouldn't start a rebellion after the captors left, they instituted the practice of large-scale deportation.

That's what happened to the Israelites of the ten northern tribes. They were marched off, fishhooks in jaws, far, far away to an area where Assyria exercised direct rule. Many perished on the way or in the new, strange lands. They disappeared from history except for a few scattered pockets that survive to our times.

So the northern kingdom was de-peopled. What did the Assyrians do next? They brought in new people—people of different ethnicity, customs, and religions—to fill the vacuum.

These became the Samaritans of Jesus' day. Ethnically, they were a mix of peoples from the Assyrian kingdom with people of Jewish descent who hadn't been deported with the others. The origin of the Samaritans is described in 2 Kings 17:24-37.

Jews looked down on these people. They despised them. And the Samaritans hated the Jews with a hatred that went back hundreds of years. The origins of the animosity constitute another chapter in the story. The Bible tells it in the books of Ezra and Nehemiah.

After the fall of the northern kingdom to the Assyrians, the kingdom of Judah in the south, tiny though it was, somehow survived for more than 100 years. It eventually succumbed, not to the Assyrians but to the Babylonians, who had supplanted the Assyrians.

The Babylonians, like the Assyrians before them, carried off the cream of Jewish society to exile, in this case to Babylon. But there something remarkable happened. In the revolving door of Middle East powers, a new giant arose—the Persians. One of their first kings, Cyrus, issued a decree that the Jews could return to their native land

and that they should be given official help to rebuild Jerusalem and the Temple, both of which the Babylonians had destroyed.

The Jews in Babylon, now in the second and third generation, had assimilated to the culture. Some had grown prosperous. They stayed put. But others packed up and made the long journey back to their homeland. They set about to rebuild the beloved city and especially the object at the heart of their religion, the Temple.

Now the story takes an interesting turn. The Samaritans heard about the plan to rebuild the Temple and showed up, offering to help in the project. But the Jews gave them the cold shoulder: they let them know that the Samaritans didn't belong. They were not Jews and they definitely were not welcome.

Later, the story takes an even sharper turn. The Jews instituted a purge. They weeded out all the non-Jewish spouses and their children from the community. They threw them out in the cold. (I personally find this one of the most distressing events in the Old Testament; read it in Ezra 10:1-44).

Get the picture with Jesus and the woman by the well? The walls separating them seem impregnable.

But Jesus wasn't your average Seventh-day Adventist. Although His ministry was spent mainly among the Jews, His words and actions made it clear that for Him walls of animosity, no matter how longstanding, didn't amount to anything. Once He healed ten lepers, one of whom was a Samaritan—the only one of the ten to say, "Thank you" (Luke 17:11-19). When Jesus was asked, "Who is our neighbor?" He told a story about a man beaten up and left for dead on the road to Jericho, and how a priest and then a Levite, passing by, saw the unfortunate fellow and crossed to the other side of the road to avoid him. The victim would have died except for a wayfarer who showed compassion on him. And the angel of mercy? He was a Samaritan.

You could almost conclude that Jesus preferred Samaritans to the religious leaders. Samaritans, rather than the clerics, come out as the good guys in the Gospels.

We usually end the story of the woman at the well with the empty water pot. The woman who came to draw water has found something far greater: "living water," new life in Christ. But that isn't all in this wonderful account. John the Gospel writer tells us later that Jesus didn't go on His way immediately—He stayed on two days with the Samaritans. Where did He sleep? Not in a Holiday Inn or a Motel 6. He slept in one of their homes! Where did He eat? Not at the local Taco Bell. He ate at a Samaritan's table!

Which, come to think of it, broke all the rules. Good Jews didn't defile themselves by going under the roof of a Gentile. Good Jews didn't eat with Gentiles. Look up the story of how Peter felt when God told him to go visit the Roman, Cornelius (Acts 10), and how later he prevaricated about eating with non-Jews when pressured by "the Brethren" (Galatians 2:11-14).

Wall #3: Hers is a different religion. The Samaritans weren't just a mongrel people; in Jewish eyes they followed a mongrel religion, a disgusting mix of Yahweh worship and paganism.

Remember how the Samaritans offered to help the Jews rebuild their Temple after they returned from Babylonian captivity? They got a strong rebuff—they weren't wanted. After that the Samaritans tried to stop work on the Temple; they tried to turn the governing authorities, right up to the king, against the project. All their efforts eventually failed, however, so what did they decide to do? They'd build their own temple, set up a rival place of worship to Jerusalem.

And they did. The Samaritans constructed a temple on Mount Gerizim and instituted a set of animal sacrifices.

This was the situation when Jesus engaged the woman in conversation. At one point in the encounter she attempted to draw Jesus into an argument about which was the place of worship—Gerizim or Jerusalem—but Jesus didn't take the bait. Instead He told her that in true worship, place doesn't matter with God: God seeks people who worship from the heart.

The religion that Jesus taught was church without walls. No walls of gender. No walls of ethnicity. No walls of codified worship.

The Jews had thrown up a high wall in their minds between them and everyone who wasn't a Jew, and in actuality their religion had its own walls.

Look at its center, the Temple. Non-Jews could only get as far as the Court of Gentiles. A sign warned them they could lose their lives if they attempted to venture beyond. Women—Jewish women—fared a bit better; they had access to the Court of Women. Jewish males were permitted to go beyond, but not all the way. To get into the Temple proper you had to have the right blood line. You had to have been born from the tribe of Levi.

But the walls didn't stop even with that. Among the Levites one family tree was singled out—the house of Aaron. Only the Aaronites could serve as priests, offering the sacrifices and entering the most sacred precincts of the Temple.

And, with all that, there was a final barrier. In the inner sanctum, the holiest place of all was kept apart, unattended. Just one individual, the High Priest, could enter it, and on only one day each year, Yom Kippur (The Day of Atonement).

Walls, walls, walls.

Jesus of Nazareth came to abolish the walls that separate humans from other humans.

Jesus came to make a church without walls.

That has to be a mark of authentic Adventism—Adventism that's true to the life and teachings of Jesus.

A church without walls.

Back to the woman by the well: yes, there's yet another wall.

Wall #4: She's a bad woman. This woman knows two things—water and men. She's someone that your average Seventh-day Adventist will be careful to steer clear of.

If your average Seventh-day Adventist happens to be a man of the cloth, he learned long ago during his internship that the Adventist Church kicks men out of the ministry for two main reasons: women and money. And the first reason is by far the more common.

But Jesus isn't too concerned about the woman's checkered past. He lets her know that He knows all about it: she's had five husbands and is now living with yet another man. He simply states the facts. No "Woman, get a grip! Your life is going down the drain. You need to do better."

The woman quickly steers the conversation onto a different topic.

It's interesting to study Jesus' encounters with bad women in the Gospels. His conversation with the Samaritan woman is by no means unique: on two other occasions the Gospel writers furnish detailed accounts of Jesus and other women with bad reputations.

Luke in chapter 7 tells how one such lady of the night interrupted a social occasion. Jesus is invited to eat at the home of a Pharisee named Simon. While they are eating, a woman sidles up to where Jesus is reclining. She breaks open a box of expensive perfume and pours it over Jesus' feet. She weeps and her tears fall over Jesus. She kisses His feet, lets down her long hair, and wipes His feet with it.

The host is scandalized. He recognizes this woman who is upsetting the dinner: she is notorious, known for her exploits with men. And he says to himself, "If Jesus were a man of God, He wouldn't let her do this. He would know what sort of person she is."

Jesus, however, doesn't tell the woman to back off. He doesn't condemn her, just as He didn't condemn the woman by the well. Instead, He tells a story that points the finger at Simon rather than the woman.

The other story takes place in the courts of the Temple (John 8: 1-11). As Jesus is teaching one morning, suddenly the religious leaders show up, dragging along a terrified woman. It's a trap: they have set up this woman in order to embarrass Jesus.

"Teacher," they smugly proclaim, "we caught this woman in bed with a man who isn't her husband. Yes, in the very act! Moses in the law taught us that adulterers should be executed—stoned to death." (Interesting: no mention of the guy she was in bed with!) "But what do you say?"

Jesus says nothing.

He stoops down and writes in the sand. He straightens up and says: "OK, let the person who is without sin himself cast the first stone." Then He writes some more.

The leaders see what He has written. One by one, as they push forward and read the words in the sand, they slink away.

Finally, only two people are left—the woman and Jesus. "Where are your accusers?" He asks. And then: "Neither do I condemn you. Go and sin no more."

What a story!

Put together these three encounters—the woman by the well, the woman at Simon's home, and the woman in the Temple—and you get a picture of Jesus that shocks. For Him there were no walls between people, no separation of "bad" people from "good" ones. He didn't care whether someone was born with a different gender or ethnic background.

Jesus' community meant church without walls.

And that's where authentic Adventism has to start.

No walls!

How are Adventists Doing?

Pretty well—but!

We're a wonderfully diverse church. In many respects we fulfill that vision of Revelation 14:6-7—a people drawn from every nation, kindred, tongue, and people. Pew Research tells the world that we are the most diverse denomination in the United States.

Wonderful! Praise God! But—

In society after society, as we spread to the ends of the earth, we took the easy road when we encountered entrenched societal patterns that warred with Jesus' message of no walls.

In India we came up against the wall of caste. What did we do? We accommodated the gospel to fit in—which meant that we distorted the message of Jesus. We set up administrative structures based on caste lines.

We have talked equality; at the 1980 General Conference Session we added a powerful new Fundamental Belief that in part states: "The church is one body with many members, called from every nation, kindred, tongue, and people. In Christ we are a new creation; distinctions of race, culture, learning, and nationality, and differences between high and low, rich and poor, male and female, must not be divisive among us. We are all equal in Christ, who by one Spirit has bonded us into one fellowship with Him and with one another; we are to serve and be served without partiality or reservation" (Fundamental Belief, #14).

Fine words! Praise God!

But easier to say than to practice.

Ethnic minorities struggle to gain their rightful place under the Adventist sun, just as they do in the larger society.

We have a hard time accepting people from other religions. From other Christian bodies? Well, maybe, but watch out for Catholics!

And when it comes to Muslims...! A good Adventist Church elder opines of the Muslims: "It would be good if we nuked all of them." Now there's a fine Christian sentiment for you.

After I retired from full-time work at the *Adventist Review*, I served for seven years as special assistant to General Conference President Jan Paulsen, tasked with developing relations with leaders of other world religions. The assignment changed my life.

We decided to start with Islam; I never got beyond that point. With multiple trips to the Middle East, my prejudices and ignorance of Muslims gradually dissipated. I came to know leaders of Islam well in both civil and religious positions. Some of these Muslims, such as the chief imam to King Abdullah of the Hashemite Kingdom of Jordan, became close friends.

After five years of encounters with Muslims, I wrote an article summarizing my conclusions. It was published in *Adventist World*, from which it went viral, bouncing around the Internet for several years. It brought more response than anything I'd written during the 24 years I edited the *Adventist Review*.

Many responses were positive, a few bewildered, but others were vitriolic: I was ignorant! I had been deceived! Didn't I know that the Muslim religion teaches them to lie? You're a disgrace to the Adventist Church!

By the time I left work among the Muslims and retired fully, a firm but sad conclusion had become embedded in my thinking: *Adventists aren't ready to welcome men and women from Islam into our churches. The Lord has large numbers of sincere followers in Islam, but the Adventist Church, as it is currently, is unable to be a channel for their salvation.*

Walls, walls, walls.

And, unfortunately, that's not all.

Publicans and Sinners

Who are the "publicans and sinners" in our times that Jesus would associate with, and be roundly criticized for doing so?

In American society, there are two. One group I have just mentioned—Muslims.

The other is people of the LGBTQ.

Many, perhaps most, of us don't know how to relate to them. Some of us do, however—they have a son or a daughter who belongs in that category.

How would Jesus relate to them? Samaritans, tax collectors, and prostitutes: He took time to talk, to sit down and eat with them. No walls.

No walls now—in authentic Adventism.

But now I need to share with you my thinking on one more wall—an Adventist wall.

Indian Summer

In regions that experience a harsh winter, the autumn sometimes brings a pleasant surprise. The days are getting shorter, the wind colder; the time of dark, of ice and snow, is coming. But then Nature abruptly changes the signals. The wind turns warm, the air dry, the sky blue. It's as though the balmy days of summer have suddenly returned.

But not for long. After a few days of warmth, winter's breath blows hard. Everyone grits their teeth at the prospect of the dark, cold months just ahead.

In North America the phenomenon is known as "Indian summer." Other continents experience similar occurrences, which they call by different names.

I'm reading news of my church, the Seventh-day Adventist Church. I read that for the year 2016 the total tithe reported for the North American Division was $1,002,276,749. More than a billion dollars. The largest total ever.

I rejoice at the generosity and faithfulness of God's people.

But then I hear a whisper: Indian summer!

Recently I read a book that sent chills up my spine: *That Was the Church That Was: How the Church of England Lost the English People* (London: Bloomsbury Centennial, 2016). It's a brutally honest examination of what caused the Church of England to lose more than half its members in the space of a decade or two. The book was written in pain: its authors, Andrew Brown and Linda Woodhead, were employed by the Church of England.

In the 1990s leaders of the church could feel pretty pleased with the way things were going. The Church of England enjoyed status as a respected plank in British society. Its finances were strong. It could boast a network of members of the Anglican Communion among countries of the former British Empire.

Leaders of the church jockeyed for position and played theological games. They were in Indian summer and didn't realize it. The grand edifice, seemingly so strong, was about to collapse like a house of cards.

What brought it down? The issue of women in ministry—at first, the issue of ordination of women as parish priests, then of women bishops.

The Church of England set up study committee after study committee, delaying decision endlessly.

Anglican women grew tired of the ecclesiastical humbug. At the very time when British society was opening its doors to new roles for women in education, church leaders were stuck in the past. They woke up too late. The talented women who all along had kept the church functioning—not just as priests but in teaching, healing, and other ministries—had left, never to return.

The picture today is a sad one: Fewer than 2 percent of the English are paying members of the church. Only one person in ten is baptized in the national church, and only one-third of the English have a church funeral.

When I read *That Was the Church That Was*, my Adventist blood ran cold.

Could it happen to us?

Are we in Indian summer?

CHAPTER FOUR

Heart Religion

Now Jesus turned to address his disciples, along with the crowd that had gathered with them. "The religion scholars and Pharisees are competent teachers in God's Law. You won't go wrong in following their teachings on Moses. But be careful about following them. They talk a good line, but they don't live it. They don't take it into their hearts and live it out in their behavior. It's all spit-and-polish veneer.

"Instead of giving you God's Law as food and drink by which you can banquet on God, they package it in bundles of rules, loading you down like pack animals. They seem to take pleasure in watching you stagger under these loads, and wouldn't think of lifting a finger to help. Their lives are perpetual fashion shows, embroidered prayer shawls one day and flowery prayers the next. They love to sit at the head table at church dinners, basking in the most prominent positions, preening in the radiance of public flattery, receiving honorary degrees, and getting called 'Doctor' and 'Reverend.'

"Don't let people do that to you, put you on a pedestal like that. You all have a single Teacher, and you are all classmates. Don't set people up as experts over your life, letting them tell you what to do. Save that authority for God; let him tell you what to do. No one else should carry the title of 'Father;'

you have only one Father, and he's in heaven. And don't let people maneuver you into taking charge of them. There is only one Life-Leader for you and them—Christ.

"Do you want to stand out? Then step down. Be a servant. If you puff yourself up, you'll get the wind knocked out of you. But if you're content to simply be yourself, your life will count for plenty.

"I've had it with you! You're hopeless, you religion scholars, you Pharisees! Frauds! Your lives are roadblocks to God's kingdom. You refuse to enter, and won't let anyone else in either.

"You're hopeless, you religion scholars and Pharisees! Frauds! You go halfway around the world to make a convert, but once you get him you make him into a replica of yourselves, double-damned.

"You're hopeless! What arrogant stupidity! You say, 'If someone makes a promise with his fingers crossed, that's nothing; but if he swears with his hand on the Bible, that's serious.' What ignorance! Does the leather on the Bible carry more weight than the skin on your hands? And what about this piece of trivia: 'If you shake hands on a promise, that's nothing; but if you raise your hand that God is your witness, that's serious'? What ridiculous hairsplitting! What difference does it make whether you shake hands or raise hands? A promise is a promise. What difference does it make if you make your promise inside or outside a house of worship? A promise is a promise. God is present, watching and holding you to account regardless.

"You're hopeless, you religion scholars and Pharisees! Frauds! You keep meticulous account books, tithing on every nickel and dime you get, but on the meat of God's Law, things like fairness and compassion and commitment—the absolute basics!—you carelessly take it or leave it. Careful bookkeeping is commendable, but the basics are required. Do you have any idea how silly you look, writing a life story that's wrong from start to finish, nitpicking over commas and semicolons?

"You're hopeless, you religion scholars and Pharisees! Frauds! You burnish the surface of your cups and bowls so they sparkle in the sun, while the insides are maggoty with your greed and gluttony. Stupid Pharisee! Scour the insides, and then the gleaming surface will mean something.

"You're hopeless, you religion scholars and Pharisees! Frauds! You're like manicured grave plots, grass clipped and the flowers bright, but six feet down it's all rotting bones and worm-eaten flesh. People look at you and think you're saints, but beneath the skin you're total frauds (Matthew 23:1-28).

Tough words from Jesus!

Matthew 23 isn't exactly an Adventist favorite. Think of all the sermons you have heard on Matthew 24—the signs of the Second Coming. How many from the chapter that immediately precedes it? I can't recall hearing even one.

Why is that?

It's not as though the topic of Matthew 23 is one that wasn't important to Jesus. Here He is, only a day or two before He's arrested, tried, and crucified. Do you think He'd devote a lengthy discourse like this to trivia?

In fact, if we go back to the beginning of Jesus' ministry we find Him emphasizing the very same ideas. Yes, right in the Sermon on the Mount. We customarily dwell on the beginning and end of that famous address, but we pass over what He says—also in strong language—in chapter 6.

In both places Jesus puts His finger on genuine religion. It's not fake. It doesn't play games. It isn't baloney.

It's heart religion.

So let's work through Matthew 23. Some of what He says may shock you; Jesus is a shocking person. Although our focus will be Matthew 23, we'll also play clips from Matthew 6 where Jesus expresses similar ideas.

Toxic Religion

In both Matthew 23 and Matthew 6 one word used by Jesus encapsulates the discussion—the Greek word *hupocrites*, literally "hypocrite." Its basic meaning is "actor," as in drama.

This word occurs seven times in Matthew 23 and three times in Matthew 6— overall, 14 times in the Gospel of Matthew. Judged by the prominence Jesus gives to this idea, we rightly conclude that playing religious games or pretending is what He finds most objectionable, most calling for rebuke, most requiring correction.

What about Adventists? How many sermons have you heard on hypocrisy—playing games in the name of God?

The Gospel of Matthew doesn't just emphasize the word "hypocrite." In both Matthew 23 and chapter 6 Jesus spells out how the hypocrites behave, giving example after example of actions by people who play religious games:

1. Talking the talk but not walking the walk

"Listen to what the religious teachers tell you," Jesus counsels His followers, "But don't do what they do. They excel in laying down the law, but they themselves don't do what they want you to do."

Words, words, words—our world is drowning in a flood of words. Information and disinformation, news and fake news, facts and alternate facts, spin doctoring, truths and half-truths, lies—what can we believe anymore? Who can we trust?

I'll tell you: People whose lives match their words. People who walk the talk. People who are *real*, not phony.

People whose religion comes from the heart.

2. Checklist religion

The religious leaders, said Jesus, pile on the rules—Don't do this. Don't do that.—until people are burdened with a heavy weight of requirements that become impossible to live up to. Religion, which should bring hope and comfort, instead means gloom and despair.

The religion of Jesus' day, Judaism, was built on Torah—divine instruction. Israel had been defeated by the armies of Babylon, the glorious Temple razed, the cream of society hauled off into exile. There, by the waters of Babylon, the Jews had lots of time to try to figure out what had gone wrong.

As they searched the books of the Old Testament, they concluded that two sins in particular had called down Yahweh's wrath: idolatry and Sabbath-breaking. They resolved to make a change; henceforth, Judaism would be a religion of strict monotheism wherein the Sabbath was kept flawlessly.

In Babylon the exiles, no longer with the Temple, developed meeting places called synagogues. They gathered together for prayers, reading of the Law, and instruction. The synagogue was a plain, austere building without ornamentation or visual representation of God. Its central element was the Torah scroll. (Readers who have attended a synagogue service will recognize the veneration accorded to the Torah scroll.)

To safeguard the Sabbath from transgression, the rabbis developed a series of regulations concerning what was permitted on the Sabbath and what was forbidden. In time these grew into a large tractate with 39 different categories. The attempt was to spell out appropriate Sabbath observance down to the smallest detail. For instance, you could only travel about two-thirds of a mile on the Sabbath—a Sabbath day's journey. If you found a scorpion in the home on Sabbath, you should cover it with a vessel and wait until the sun set to kill it.

Religion that centers in rules, trying to specify conduct for every circumstance of life, inevitably becomes self-defeating. Life is too complicated to be held fast within ironclad rules. So the rabbis had to come up with exceptions to the rules. Yes, you could only travel two-thirds of a mile on the Sabbath, but if on Friday you left a cache of food along the way, on Sabbath you could eat that food and then you're setting out on a new journey! (Compare Orthodox Jews' Sabbath keeping today: they are not permitted to turn on the light switch, but it's fine if a Gentile turns it on for them.)

The focus on rules eventually led to a huge compendium of dos and don'ts. At first this body of extra-biblical material, known as Halakal, was transmitted orally, but in the third century AD it was reduced to writing in the work known as the Mishnah. Reflection, discussion, and argument among the competing schools of rabbinical interpretation continued for several more centuries. Eventually the work came to a close in the Talmud. (The Babylonian Talmud ran to some 70 volumes; the Palestinian Talmud was shorter.)

This checklist religion was too demanding for the common people; their life focused on putting bread on the table twice a day. Only the religious leaders—the scribes and Pharisees—had the time and the means to adhere to the stringent demands of the Law. And they in turn looked down on the common people. "This mob that knows nothing of the law—there is a curse on them," they stated (John 7:49, NIV).

Jesus ran afoul of the checklist religion of His day. He flouted the traditions taught by the scribes and Pharisees. They hated Him and quite soon recognized Him as a threat to their control over the people. The people loved Him; the religious leaders saw Him as a dangerous rabble-rouser.

3. All for show

"They do all their deeds to be seen by others," Jesus said of the religious leaders of His day (Matthew 23:5, ESV). In the Sermon on the Mount He blasted them for their religious baloney: standing on the street corners and making long prayers for everyone to see and be impressed, making a public show of their charitable gifts, and disfiguring their faces to let others know that they were fasting.

They have already received their reward, Jesus said—the praise they get from on-lookers, awe-struck by their supposed piety. But that is the only reward they'll get. The Father in heaven isn't impressed by their games. He sees what they're up to; the approval that they seek stops right here on earth.

Sobering words! Why do I do what I do as a follower of Jesus? My Sabbath-keeping? My tithes and offerings? My charitable gifts? What if the IRS changed its policy and no longer permitted me to report my gifts as tax-deductible? Would I continue to give?

The scribes and Pharisees made a show of their religiosity even by the way they dressed. Way back in the Law of Moses the Lord spoke about binding the Law close to one's person, to meditate on it, to talk about it with family members (see Deuteronomy 6:6-8). Whether or not Yahweh meant the instruction about binding to be taken literally, the religious leaders certainly did. They let the world see how pious they were by sewing wide hems in their robes and parading big phylacteries (small cases that contained portions of the Law written on parchment).

All for show! All to impress others!

But Jesus counseled His disciples, and He counsels us: "Beware of practicing your piety before others in order to be seen by them; for then you have no reward from your Father in heaven" (Matthew 6:1, NRSV). When you give, keep the act to yourself, especially if it is a large offering. Do it so quietly and secretly that, as it were, your left hand won't know what your right hand has done. When you pray, pray from the heart, alone, just you and God. And no need to rattle on about all you think you need: the Father knows already what you really need. Likewise when you decide to fast: It's between you and God. Don't tell anyone what you're doing. It's a secret between you and the Father. And the Father will see in secret and be delighted.

4. Toxic religion

Religion that focuses on rules becomes toxic. It's dangerous to spiritual health—yours and others' with whom you come into contact.

Legalistic religion concerns itself with behavior, not people. It puts rules above fellowship. It puts Law above God.

Legalistic religion becomes dry, arid, and judgmental. If you go down that road, you become proud of how much better you are than other poor dimwits who don't keep all the rules like you. So you become puffed up in your religiosity—how great you must be in God's sight—and judgmental of others.

Toxic religion is dangerous. It makes you sick spiritually and spreads to others who are worshiping with you.

Jesus told stories that make that point with piercing clarity. Like the story of the two men who went up to the Temple to pray.

One was a Pharisee. His prayer went like this: I thank you, God, that I'm not like other people. I fast, I return tithes diligently, I'm really a wonderful person! And I thank you that I'm not like *that* person—that tax collector! What's he doing here in Your house, anyway? Surely he doesn't belong here!"

The tax collector's prayer was short. Falling on his knees before God, he simply confessed his sins and asked God to be merciful toward him.

And, Jesus said, when the two men left the Temple and went home, only one prayer had been heard: the tax collector's.

5. Titles and perks

The religious leaders reveled in titles. They loved to be called "rabbi," which means "teacher," "father," and "guide." A plain "mister" wouldn't have been good enough to satisfy their egos. (There was no "missus"—the scribes and Pharisees belonged to an exclusive all-male club.)

In that society, where the Temple and its services were the high point of the social order and life centered in religion, religious leaders enjoyed a privileged place. Religious office came with perks. When you went to the synagogue or you were invited to a social event, the host always ushered you to the head table.

Yes, religion was about God—but for its leaders, it was about far more.

For Jesus, that was all humbug. It missed the essence, which deals with the heart, in sincere worship of the one God and love for one's fellow men and women.

After the searing condemnation of the religious leaders, recorded in Matthew 23:1-12, Jesus pronounced seven woes on them. "Woe to you, scribes and Pharisees, hypocrites!" Strong, powerful words: but there were tears in Jesus' voice.

6. Woe to you—keeping people out of the kingdom

Your religion is toxic. It's deadly; it kills. It will keep you out of the kingdom of heaven, and it keeps others out too. You are supposed to be a teacher, a guide to God's people, but your teachings result in exactly the opposite of what God wants.

Woe, woe, indeed.

7. Woe to you—winning souls for your own ego, not for the Kingdom of heaven

As the Jews spread across the Roman Empire, the positive features of their religion, such as strict monotheism and moral living that contrasted with the dissipations of the prevailing culture, attracted thoughtful Gentiles. Some just attended synagogue services, but others went all the way to embrace Judaism. They were called "God fearers," and Paul encountered many of them during his missionary tours. Other Gentiles, however, actually submitted to the rites that made them a proselyte—ritual baptism and circumcision.

The Pharisees of Jesus' day viewed these proselytes as human trophies. They worked on them to bring them into line with their legalistic adherence to Torah. They wanted the proselytes to behave just as they did.

Thus, even in "soul-winning"—to use a good Adventist expression—the religious leaders distorted genuine religion. Their activities that were focused on the proselytes were actually all about them, the scribes and Pharisees, not about God.

The Lord, however, isn't impressed by such "soul winning." For God, it isn't so much a matter of how many people we baptize but rather how many of these people are members of the Kingdom of God.

8. Woe to you—promises, promises

The religious leaders excelled in casuistry: they made rules but invented means of circumventing the rules. You could make a promise, but maybe they'd show you a way out of keeping your word.

Let's say you own a piece of real estate and are ready to sell it. You set the price at 500 denarii. A buyer shows up.

"Are you really selling that property for 500?"

"Sure am."

'That's a good price. Can I be sure you won't change your mind while I arrange the finances?"

"Trust me. Listen, I'll swear on it. I swear by the Temple that the price is 500 denarii."

The buyer goes away to work on the money. Then someone else comes along.

"I hear you're selling your property. I've been hoping to obtain it for a long while. Listen, I really want it. I'll give you 600 denarii to make it mine."

Now you're sorry. You could have sold it for so much more than you're getting.

What to do? No worries: the religious leader comes to your rescue. You tell him the situation. He says, "You swore by the Temple, right?"

"Yes."

"So tell me: Did you swear by the Temple in general or by the gold of the Temple?"

"By the Temple."

"It's your lucky day. You don't have to keep your promise!"

Junk religion! Casuistry! Baloney!

Jesus said: "I want you to be people who are true to your word, who keep promises. No need to swear by the Temple or anything. 'Yes' and 'No' should be good enough for you."

Come to think of it, why do some people say, "Trust me" before they pass on information? Isn't their word good enough without that?

Or "Believe me." Maybe that's a signal that we ought to be careful about believing them!

9. Woe to you—majoring in minors, minoring in majors

Tithing is a good practice; it comes from God. The religious leaders wanted to make sure that they did it right. Their rules went into great length about how to tithe the figs on the tree in your garden. Some even counted the leaves of the garden herbs—on mint, dill, and cumin—and plucked off every tenth one to be returned as tithe.

"You are so careful about tithing," Jesus said, "and that's good—you should return tithe. But you have it all wrong—you're meticulous in tithing but blind to things that count far more. Justice, mercy, and faith are what really matter with God."

Their scale of values was upside down. They had focused on minutiae so long that they couldn't see the woods for the trees. They strained out a gnat from the water they drank, but gulped down a camel!

10. Woe to you—focusing on externals but neglecting the heart

For you, it's all about externals.

How you look.

What other people think about you.

What they say about you.

So pious.

So close to God.

If people only knew what you're really like! Inside your long robes with their big phylacteries, God sees that your religion is all about you—your greed, your selfishness.

11. Woe to you—unmindful of how repulsive you are to God

You are like those monuments on the hills erected over the tombs of the prophets. They gleam white in the sunlight, but just open up the vault! It stinks of rotting flesh.

Listen, you are in a *bad, bad* way spiritually. Your problem is made worse because you look and act so pious. Your religion is one big act, one game after another. And the Law you talk so much about: You bash other people over the head with it, but how about you? Do you keep it yourselves? No, you don't!

12. Woe to you—the sins of the fathers

You like to think how much better you are than your fathers. They killed the prophets—nothing you'd think of doing.

Really? You are about to commit a sin far worse than anything the old-timers did. Already in your hearts you're plotting it. You plan to murder the One who is the greatest of the prophets.

You are a bunch of snakes! On your way to hell!

Wow!

Can this be Jesus—the gentle Jesus, meek and mild?

This is Jesus, telling it like it is.

Telling it with tears in His voice.

Whatever does this chapter have for Adventists today? A lot, if we have ears to hear.

Matthew 23 and Adventists

Let's be clear from the start: Jesus' stern words addressed to the scribes and Pharisees are meant for all of us. We shouldn't distort them to apply only to the religious leaders among us—pastors, presidents of conferences, union conferences, divisions, General Conference officers. At the same time, however, those in leadership roles do have added accountability. God intends that they should be shepherds of the flock, spiritual guides to help us all in the road to the kingdom.

I believe that everyone who takes seriously the life and teachings of Jesus of Nazareth should ponder prayerfully His counsel in Matthew 23 and Matthew 6. Ask yourself, "Could this be me? Is my religion from the heart? Is it toxic? Is the church I attend toxic?

Yes, friends, there are toxic churches. Some Adventist churches should post a sign: *Danger: Toxic religion practiced here.*

I'm not exaggerating. Let me tell you about one.

For many years our family used to spend vacations at a favorite beach. A lot of other Adventists did the same. Way back someone came up with the idea of renting a church building from a "Sunday" church and holding Sabbath services for all the Adventists relaxing at the beach. It was a great plan; for years many of us enjoyed fellowship and worship in a Lutheran church with beautiful stained glass windows. It was a transient summer congregation. After the days turned cold and the vacationers left, Sabbath services came to an end.

Then a couple of Adventist families retired in the area and began to keep the church open year-round. They worked to grow the congregation. From time to time I was invited to speak to them.

Slowly the group grew to 10, 20, and finally about 30.

Noelene and I rejoiced at what we saw happening as from time to time I was asked to speak to the growing congregation. It was small but warm, small but inviting.

After a lapse of several months, we made another visit. We sensed it immediately—something had happened. We felt judged and found wanting. Some legalistic Adventists had moved into the area and wormed their way into leadership roles. They had taken over the church.

Their attitude was toxic. Wary of anyone coming from big, bad Washington, they wanted to keep their group small and pure. Noelene and I were intruding on their "club."

Who do we think we're fooling when we think like that?

What happened to the little church? You can guess. Legalists killed it. Oh, that this were an isolated example; sadly, it isn't.

Case #1: We visit our hometown in Australia and meet up with a lovely young Adventist woman, a dear friend. She confides in us: she's fallen in love and wants to marry. But the guy isn't Adventist!

She asks the conference youth leader to perform the wedding ceremony. He says: "If I officiate, I'll be out of the ministry because Adventists are supposed to only marry Adventists."

But he goes on: "There is a way I can get involved. If you drop your membership in the church, then you'll be like your fiancé and I'm allowed to officiate at the wedding!"

I find this extraordinary. I understand and support the Adventist Church's advocating that couples be of the same faith, but which is the greater value—marriage itself or both partners being Adventist? In today's society where the majority of young people move in together before getting married, shouldn't we make marriage the priority, encouraging and supporting it?

Our young friend didn't quit the Adventist Church. She and her fiancé found a minister of another denomination to preside at their wedding. When it came time to dedicate the first child, where do you think it felt most natural for them to go?

Case #2: This one is painfully personal.

It's the dark days of the great economic Depression of the 1930s. Work is hard to find, money harder.

My parents have nine kids—yes, nine! I'm the youngest, born right in the middle of the hard times.

Dad scratches and claws, finds a job now and then, starts a little business. He has money—a little—in his pocket.

The kids need shoes.

Dad, an earnest convert to Adventism, decides to take the little money he has and return a tenth. Goodbye shoes.

Mom, who has not joined him on his journey into the Adventist Church, is furious. Years later she recounts the story with bitterness.

As I write these words, after so many years, I think of my godly father and for the first time in my life I wonder: Did he do the right thing? He returned the tithe; that is good. So is putting shoes on the feet of your kids. Did he neglect the "weightier matters" of Matthew 23: justice, mercy, and faith?

Did my godly father major in minors and minor in majors?

Authentic Religion

Matthew 23—what a chapter!

A wonderful, upsetting, scary chapter.

Matthew 23 rakes across my heart, scattering the leaves, stirring the debris accumulated there.

The scribes and Pharisees: Watch out, Bill Johnsson! Don't come down on the religious leaders of a bygone age before you look hard into your own heart!

CHAPTER FIVE

Transparent as Light

The next day Jesus decided to go to Galilee. When he got there, he ran across Philip and said, "Come, follow me." (Philip's hometown was Bethsaida, the same as Andrew and Peter.)

Philip went and found Nathanael and told him, "We've found the One Moses wrote of in the Law, the One preached by the prophets. It's Jesus, Joseph's son, the one from Nazareth!" Nathanael said, "Nazareth? You've got to be kidding."

But Philip said, "Come, see for yourself."

When Jesus saw him coming he said, "There's a real Israelite, not a false bone in his body."

Nathanael said, "Where did you get that idea? You don't know me."

Jesus answered, "One day, long before Philip called you here, I saw you under the fig tree."

Nathanael exclaimed, "Rabbi! You are the Son of God, the King of Israel!"

Jesus said, "You've become a believer simply because I say I saw you one day sitting under the fig tree? You haven't seen anything yet! Before this is over you're going to see heaven open and God's angels descending to the Son of Man and ascending again" (John 1:43-51).

Nathaniel was Jesus' sort of person.

You could trust this man. You could buy a used car from him and be confident that he hadn't turned back the odometer or doctored the vehicle just to get you to buy it.

Of Nathaniel Jesus said, as soon as He laid eyes on him, "Here is truly an Israelite in whom there is no deceit." The word for "deceit" is *dolos* in the Greek, which is translated "guile" in the KJV. The basic meaning of *dolos* is "bait." It's a term from fishing. The angler puts on the hook a worm, or some other morsel that the fish thinks is delicious, and dangles it in front of the fish. The fish takes a look, swims around, comes back, nibbles—and takes the bait.

That's *dolos*, "deceit," "guile," "pretense." And in today's world it's used by a whole lot more than fishermen.

Advertising, so big a part of our culture, to a large degree uses *dolos*. Whatever the product, from BMWs to Bud Light, it comes packaged with voluptuous women, everyone looking confident and happy.

The message is: You're not just buying a product. You're buying happiness, prestige, self-worth.

Dangle, dangle, dangle. The bait looks irresistible.

Nathaniel—no bait. No hook. No hidden agenda.

With Nathaniel, what you see is what you get.

Authentic Adventists will be like Nathaniel. Jesus liked what He saw. He called Nathaniel a true Israelite. Search through the four Gospels and you won't find Jesus using this language about anyone else.

What did Jesus mean by it?

To try to figure it out, you have to go back to the first Israelite, whose given name was Jacob.

Jacob was—no other way to say it—a crook. The Book of Genesis devotes several chapters to telling his story, and it's not a pretty tale.

At every point along his journey, you find him lying and deceiving. He thinks he's being clever.

The truth is: He's way too clever by half.

The day will come when this crook, this manipulator, this liar will get his come-uppance. You can feel it coming. You just know that Jacob's day of reckoning will come.

And when it comes—Wow! Does the roof ever cave in on poor lying Jacob! I can't help but chuckle as I think of it.

How bad was Jacob? Really, really bad.

He tricked his twin brother Esau into bartering away the place of honor as firstborn in the family. (They were twins, but Esau was older by moments.) Jacob thought that the spiritual blessing that the birthright was meant to be could be treated like a barrel of oil that could be bought or sold.

But there's more: he tricked his old, blind father. He lied and lied, pretending to be Esau. The poor man, eyesight shot, hearing also bad, became confused. Who was this person who sounded like Jacob but insisted that he was Esau?

At last the old man was convinced: it had to be Esau. He gave Jacob the blessing that he intended Esau to have.

Jacob, so cunning!

Jacob, so low down!

It's despicable, playing tricks on your own father. Can he sink any lower than that?

The trickster didn't get to enjoy his "success." Esau found out and vowed: "My brother's gonna die! I'll wait until Dad is off the scene, and then…"

Jacob fled. He headed north, far, far away where he'd be safe from his murderous brother. He was homeless, penniless, friendless.

This was what all his lying and deceitfulness brought him.

Weary from the trek, he got ready to spend the night in the wild. No sleeping bag, no blanket, no camp cot.

No pillow. He looked around and found a large stone that would have to do for his head. He fell asleep.

The stars came out. He had a dream, a dream about God. It's a stairway to paradise with angels going up and down, and above it all he sees Yahweh.

Suddenly he was wide awake. The thought stuck him like a lightning bolt: "God is here—even here! He's not just back in the land of my people. He's here! I'm not alone."

Then the trickster, coming off this night of revelation, made a promise to the God who had come to him in the dream. But even as he made the promise, he couldn't quite get beyond the old tricky Jacob.

His promise went like this: "God, if You will look after me and bring me back safe to my family home, I promise to give back to You one tenth of everything I earn."

Some promise! *If…!* The trickster couldn't help himself: it had to be a bargain. He had to come out with the best end of it.

He went on his way, trying, I imagine, to get the crick out of his aching neck. (That "pillow" was hard!) On and on he went, hundreds of miles, until he arrived in the northwest—Iraq in today's world.

Was Jacob glad to arrive! And he was even more glad when he came upon a pretty girl herding her father's sheep.

She was beautiful. Something jumped within his weary heart.

Thus began a new chapter in the trickster's story. It became the saga of Jacob, Rachel whom he loved, and her father, Laban.

What poor Jacob didn't know was that he had fallen into the hands of someone every bit as cunning and deceitful as he was. If Jacob was a piece of work, multiply that by 10 and you get Laban.

Jacob was sure of it—Rachel was the only one for him. He asked Laban for her hand.

"OK," said Laban, "but what can you pay for her? That's the custom in these parts: the groom brings a bride price."

Jacob was broke.

But Laban came to the rescue: "No worries, my friend. I'll tell you what to do: simply work for me seven years and I'll keep your wages. That will be your bride price."

(Did I warn you about Laban?)

Some deal. But Jacob was smitten with Rachel. If he had to work without pay for seven years but then got Rachel, so be it. He agreed.

The years hurried by. They raced faster and faster. Soon he'd have Rachel as his bride.

Cut to the wedding. The bride was as pretty as a peach—surely she was, underneath all the thick veils of her wedding outfit.

At last all the hoop-la, all the celebrations, were over. The guests went home. Jacob went to his tent with Rachel.

To keep it kosher we pass over the rest of that night. When daylight seeped in next morning, Jacob turned to look at his new wife, lovely without all the material clutter of the night before.

He looked. He rubbed his eyes.

"Rachel," he said. "You sure look different in the morning. Rachel? Rachel!

"WHO ARE YOU?"

"I'm Leah, Rachel's sister."

Leah! Jacob reached for his iPhone.

"Laban, what's going on? There's been a big mistake!"

"Now my boy, calm down. What's the problem?"

"It's Rachel—no, it's *not* Rachel in my bed. That's the problem. Someone switched my bride in the night. I ended up with Leah."

"Oh, really? Not surprising. Leah, eh? Listen, everything is in order. In our country a younger sister is not allowed to marry before the older. So what happened is all quite normal."

"But I love Rachel. I gave seven backbreaking years for her! When do I get my bride?"

"Take it easy, my son. It's all quite simple. Now that Leah's married, you can have Rachel whenever you wish. If you're so upset, we can even put on another wedding right away."

"Great! So Rachel and I will be married after all."

"Of course, trust me: But you realize, I hope, that you'll have to pay for her."

"What?"

"Yes, a simple matter. Just work for me another seven years. I'll keep your wages as the bride price!"

Seven more years. Jacob had been snookered. The chickens had returned home to roost.

Jacob's home life developed into a disaster. His two wives, sisters, fought like cats. They maneuvered for his affection; they used kids as pawns in the marriage game. They introduced more women into the household—secondary wives.

The trickster now had a house with four warring women and kids everywhere. The lies and deceit continued. It was the quintessential dysfunctional marriage, a marriage from hell.

The sins of the father passed down to the kids. Lies and deceit. A really dark element surfaced: violence, incest, murder.

All the time relations with father-in-law Laban went from bad to worse. Jacob and Laban schemed and plotted to outdo the other. Jacob would have packed up and left except he had no place to go: he had burned his bridges back in Canaan. Angry Esau was waiting to kill him.

Finally Jacob could stand life with Laban no longer. He was getting out: better to try his luck with Esau than put up with conniving Laban one more day. But after he reached the decision he resorted to his true form: instead of leaving in an honorable fashion that would allow Laban to kiss his grandchildren goodbye, Jacob and family decided to sneak away, heading south. And when they did so, the lovely Rachel stole Laban's household gods and lied about it.

What a family!

Right near the close of his life, Jacob ended up in Egypt. Chatting with Jacob, Pharaoh inquired about Jacob's age, to which the patriarch replied: "The years of my earthly sojourn are one hundred thirty; few and hard have been the years of my life" (Genesis 47:9, NRSV). To me, 130 seems like a pretty good inning, but poor old lying Jacob could only think that he had been a failure.

If Jacob's story ended there, it would be a sad, sad tale of a crook who got what he deserved. But there's another part to the story, an element that transforms it.

Jacob was heading south with his family and flocks, leaving Laban and Haran far behind. As he approached home after so long a time, one person consumed his being—Esau! He now must face the brother who had threatened to kill him. And now he got word that Esau was coming with a band of armed men.

Distressed, Jacob knew his only possible help was in Yahweh. He spent the night alone by the brook Jabbok, seeking the God who had appeared to him long ago when he fled from Esau. During the night, in the darkness, something wild happened. Suddenly he was attacked: an unknown assailant was trying to kill him. Jacob fought desperately for his life.

It was a life-and-death struggle. At last, just before dawn, Jacob realized that his opponent wasn't just a robber after all. There was something strange, something supernatural about him. Then as the being struggled to escape, Jacob cried out: "I won't let you go until you bless me!"

This was Jacob at the end of his tether. No more bargaining with God. Jacob cried out for help from the depths of despair.

Yes, it was God. Not the God of the angels ascending and descending, but the God of struggle who comes to us in our hour of desperate need.

Jacob would never be the same after this night by the Jabbok. And as evidence that he was a changed person, Yahweh gave him a new name, Israel, which means "prince of God" or "overcomer."

Jacob to Israel.

From liar to prince.

This is grace.

In subsequent generations the Hebrews would refer to themselves as "children of Israel." Not "children of Abraham." Not "children of Isaac." Not "children of Joseph."

Think of it: children of tricky Jacob, but no longer tricky Jacob. Instead—Israel!

The land of the Jews today might have been called "Abraham," "Isaac," or "Joseph." No, it's "Israel"!

That's how the first Israelite came into being. And that's what Jesus saw in Nathanael—a true Israelite, a true prince of God.

Not a sneaky, lying, deceitful person like Jacob. But a new person—a person born of God.

A person honest and straightforward, true.

A person transparent in all their ways.

Seventh-day Adventists, are we true Israelites? Or is Jacob looking over our shoulder? Let's turn the searchlight on ourselves.

Topsy-Turvy Times

We live in weird, topsy-turvy times. We're being swept away by a tsunami of information. Worse, rational discourse is out the window. News, fake news; facts, alternate facts; spin, lies; talk, talk, talk—what is up and what is down anymore?

At such a time as this Jesus calls His followers to live honestly, openly, straightforwardly, transparently. He calls us individually; He calls us corporately.

I recall vividly the shock I felt when, years ago, a brother holding a major position in the Adventist Church shared a juicy morsel of denominational scandal and followed it with: "If you quote me on this, I'll deny before God that I ever said it!"

I'm still shocked.

What is this parsing of truth and falsehood? If I tell you that I am going to lie, does that make it no longer a lie?

I don't think so. To me that sort of reasoning is a page out of the scribes' legalistic, casuistic games.

It doesn't fit with the life and teachings of Jesus. He was, says the beloved Gospel writer John, "full of grace and truth" (John 1:14).

Truth—full of it.

We like the "full of grace" part. Can we abide the "full of truth" bit that comes with it?

Fact is, Jesus spoke quite a lot about truth. "You will know the truth, and the truth will set you free," He told the Jews (John 8:32). He said that He came to earth to point out the truth in the midst of the devil's lies. When He stood before Pilate in the judgment hall, the confrontation was all about truth. "I have come to bear witness to the truth," He said. To which the Roman governor gave a cynical rejoinder, "What is truth?" (John 18:38).

What is truth, indeed?

Jesus is truth, He is THE TRUTH. "I am the way, the truth, and the life," He told the Twelve on that last Thursday night (John 14:6).

How far I fall short of that standard! How far my church falls short of it!

I'm talking with a colleague. We talk for a while, but I sense that somehow we're not connecting. We understand each other's words, but something is missing.

At last he comes straight out with it: "I'm trying to figure out the subtext of this conversation."

"Subtext"?

"Yes, I'm not clear about the meaning behind your words."

I tell him, "There's no subtext. I try to say just what I mean."

That's how I grew up. Australians are direct in their conversation, far more so than Americans. At times they're blunt, bordering on rudeness. Their speech lacks the subtlety, the diplomacy, of discourse here.

Of course, each culture has its strengths and its weaknesses. Above all else, I want my communication to be like Nathanael's— without *dolos*, without deceit.

On the Knife-Edge

For a quarter century the Adventist Church entrusted me with a major responsibility, the editorship of the church's flagship jour-nal, the *Adventist Review*. It's one of the oldest journals published in America; it was the first endeavor of our movement. Founded by James White, the paper from the outset was more than just a journal of information. It was a lively paper in which differing viewpoints of doctrine were exchanged, often vigorously. At times the editors spoke with a prophetic voice, as when they called on Adventists to disobey the fugitive slave law that required anyone who found a runaway slave to return the slave to the owner.

That is a noble heritage. I am proud of it. To be entrusted with guiding the *Review*, as only the tenth editor in its long existence, was an assignment that I took very seriously.

For most of its existence, the *Review* was published by the Review and Herald Publishing Association; editors were employees of the publishing house. First in Battle Creek and then in Washington, DC, the publishing house and the General Conference were located in ad-jacent buildings. Thus, the *Review* served the Adventist Church as a vehicle closely cooperating with the General Conference but main-taining a healthy distance from it.

All that changed in 1982 when the publishing house relocated to Hagerstown, MD. Now the question arose: Should the church pa-per move out of Washington along with the house, or should it be at-tached to the General Conference? The issue was vigorously debated at a Spring Meeting of the General Conference, with some delegates warning that if the paper were to come under the General Confer-ence, it would become a PR journal, "a Pravda," as one notable leader put it.

The vote went in favor of keeping the *Review* in Washington, DC. Its editors switched from being employees of the house to those of the General Conference.

I took over the editor's chair exactly when the change went into effect. Conscious of the rich heritage of respectful distance from the General Conference leadership, I determined to try to prevent the paper from becoming a house organ for the General Conference.

At times I succeeded; others, not so well. In general the three bosses I reported to in turn—General Conference Presidents Neal C. Wilson, Robert Folkenberg, and Jan Paulson—left us free to do our job without hindrance. None of them ever told us what we must print or not print.

An ongoing question involved the bad news. No problem with the good news, of which there was plenty, but what about scandals and corruption, which inevitably take place in every human organization? Should we turn a blind eye? Should we spin doctor them? Or should we share the truth—painful, perhaps embarrassing—with the people?

I believed and still believe that the people have a right to know. When things go wrong, Adventists shouldn't have to find out from a secular newspaper.

I believe that our people can handle the truth. What they cannot abide is lies.

Sometimes at the Review office I walked a knife-edge. To publish or not to publish? The buck stopped at my desk. It drove me to my knees for wisdom—and courage.

In the office we became aware of an ugly, distasteful problem among Adventists—sexual abuse. Back then we didn't realize how pervasive it was in all churches. The dirty secret seemed too shameful to be brought into the open.

For several years we pondered the matter, trying to figure out when and how to break the news to the people. We knew it would be a bombshell.

Every autumn, leaders of the church in North America gathered for discussions. We introduced the plan of putting on a dinner for them, followed by a free-ranging discussion. At last the year came when a union president, somewhat hesitantly, shared his conviction that the church needed to tackle its well-kept secret. Others agreed; we had the green light.

We published an article. It brought a flood of letters from abused women—the dam broke. We followed up with an entire issue devoted to the topic, no holds barred.

Not everyone was happy. "Cancel my subscription," wrote some subscribers. "I'm ashamed for my mail carrier to read what you are putting in the *Review*. Shame on you!"

But what we did was right.

Telling the truth is always right.

Another sad situation tested our mettle. The Adventist Church president became entangled in financial dealings with a crook who then blackmailed him. Only a couple of people at the General Conference knew about it, Treasurer Bob Rawson and Chief Legal Counsel Bob Nixon. They stood tall. They refused to agree to the money-laundering scheme that the president wanted in order to keep the crook off his back. The crook sued, and named the General Conference. The fat was in the fire.

I was informed very early about the impending crisis. Still reeling from the shock, I called the staff together for a closed-door meeting. I informed them that news was about to break that would rock the church. How would the *Review* handle it?

We bound ourselves to a list of protocols for our coverage. Tell the news openly, candidly, accurately. Get it out fast. Include a redemptive perspective to help readers cope.

Events moved fast. Exactly two months after the new broke, the General Conference president was gone and a new leader elected to office. For each of the big three developments along the way, we tore up the issue we'd planned, wrote new copy, and rushed the issue into print. We printed our story—not the official release from the General Conference Communication Department.

The people can handle the truth. The church moved ahead, hardly missing a beat.

The Washington, DC, Environment

Congress has fallen on sorry times. Manipulation, secrecy, and win-at-any-cost seem to have become normal. A small group works in secret, crafting legislation that will affect the lives of millions. Details are kept secret, only released with insufficient time to examine the legislation. Ram the bill through. Cut off debate. Just secure a majority vote—a one-vote majority will be fine.

The General Conference is located in this environment. Inevitably, the machinations of politicians impact leaders at world headquarters. The evils of processes in Congress leak down and pervert the councils of the Adventist Church.

I call the leaders at the General Conference and all sections of the church to transparency:

No secret sessions.

No manipulation of process.

No restricting of sufficient time for delegates to discuss and debate.

No declaring important items passed by razor-thin majorities. If an item after debate fails to win a consensus, withdraw it and continue to work on it.

This is the church, my church.

This is authentic Adventism.

Let the little woman with the prophetic voice have the last word.

"Everything that Christians do should be as transparent as the sunlight. Truth is of God; deception, in every one of its myriad forms, is of Satan; and whoever in any way departs from the straight line of truth is betraying himself into the power of the wicked one" (Ellen White, *Thoughts from the Mount of Blessing*, p. 68).

CHAPTER SIX

Present Truth

On the final and climactic day of the Feast, Jesus took his stand. He cried out, "If anyone thirsts, let him come to me and drink. Rivers of living water will brim and spill out of the depths of anyone who believes in me this way, just as the Scripture says." (He said this in regard to the Spirit, whom those who believed in him were about to receive. The Spirit had not yet been given because Jesus had not yet been glorified.) (John 7:37-39, MSG).

"I still have many things to tell you, but you can't handle them now. But when the Friend comes, the Spirit of the Truth, he will take you by the hand and guide you into all the truth there is. He won't draw attention to himself, but will make sense out of what is about to happen and, indeed, out of all that I have done and said. He will honor me; he will take from me and deliver it to you. Everything the Father has is also mine. That is why I've said, 'He takes from me and delivers to you'" (John 16:12-15).

One of the factors that attracted me to Adventism—and which still attracts me—is its openness to truth.

For Ellen White and the other pioneers, truth was progressive. Never static. Not cut and dried. The following statement from her pen is typical: "There is no excuse for anyone in taking the position that there is no more truth to be revealed, and that all our expositions of Scripture are without an error. The fact that certain doctrines have been held as truth for many years by our people, is not a proof that our ideas are infallible. Age will not make error into truth, and truth can afford to be fair. No true doctrine will lose anything by close investigation" (*Counsels to Writers and Editors*, p. 35).

The apostle Peter's words encapsulated their conviction: "For this reason I will not be negligent to remind you always of these things, though you know and are established in the present truth" (2 Peter 1:12, NKJV).

Present truth—that says it all. Not truth from yesterday, not truth from Martin Luther, important though it was in its own time and will always be. Not truth from the Anglicans, the Methodists, the Baptists, the Presbyterians, but *present* truth, truth for today.

Truth that is alive. Truth that is fresh. Truth that comes to us from the womb of the dawn. Truth that sparkles with the dewdrops of heaven.

Truth that comes from the utterance of the Holy Spirit.

So important was this idea to the pioneers of our faith that they strenuously resisted any effort to capture Adventism in a creedal statement. One term expressed the way they thought of themselves: movement. "Movement" indicated progress, change, openness to the Spirit's leading into all truth.

Not a church—a *movement*.

Because of this conviction, this fervent desire to be ready to learn and embrace the new, they resisted organization in all forms. Organization, they argued, would bring a slowing down and eventual stagnation. It would lead to Adventists becoming like the other churches—satisfied with their distinctive teachings derived from their pioneers, but no longer a vital, dynamic body advancing in the light of the Spirit.

Inevitably, organization became necessary. The believers were few and scattered; they were "the little flock scattered abroad," as one of Ellen White's earliest writings described them.

James White saw the need of organization. Against fierce opposition, with those on the other side proclaiming "Babylon!" he led the Adventist believers first to adopt an official name, Seventh-day Adventist, and then to be legally registered.

We grew. And grew. And grew. The little flock morphed at length into a worldwide church of some 20 million. Organization, once a dirty word, became the watchword.

According to SDA historian George Knight, Adventists now are the most organized ("bureaucratic") church in existence, on a par with the Roman Catholic Church. For a body that started out as a movement fiercely opposed to organization, the change is startling. From no organization we became super-organized.

The size of the organization isn't the main thing, however. What is more important is whether organization gets in the way of the Spirit's working.

Newcomers to the General Conference Committee are surprised, as I was, to learn how the church goes about its business at the highest levels. Every item that comes before the Annual Council has already traveled through a series of committees that may stretch back two or more years. When the item at last comes up for consideration, a line at the top indicates the different steps where it has been vetted. The role of the Annual Council is to vote on what has already been processed by other groups.

This precedence is especially true of the highest deliberative body, the General Conference Session. A delegate may arrive feeling passionately about some matter that he or she feels warrants discussion by the world church, but they go home disappointed. Only items processed and discussed already make it on the agenda.

I understand the need for careful discussion of items ahead of the Session. What might be the result if the 2,000 plus delegates were permitted to introduce new items from the floor? The potential for disorder would be high—and we Adventists love that text: "Let all things be done decently and in order" (1 Corinthians 14:40, KJV). A highly sensitive matter might be debated and, in the heat of the moment, secure a majority vote, with perhaps disastrous consequences for the long-term good of the church.

We play it safe and, as a general rule, I think wisely so.

And yet...

What part does the Holy Spirit play? What part do we *permit* the Spirit to play?

I read the Book of Acts and the contrast between then and now hits me between the eyes. Over and over the Spirit speaks to individuals, sometimes to a local church, and individuals act on the divine Voice and go forward. The Spirit speaks to Peter, and he leaves Joppa and goes to the home of the Gentile centurion Cornelius. The Spirit speaks to Philip, and he heads south and catches up with the Ethiopian courtier. The Spirit speaks to Paul and Barnabas and "forbids" them to preach the gospel in the Roman provinces of Asia, and then Bithynia. And then the Spirit, by means of a dream, speaks again, instructing them to take the gospel to Macedonia.

All these instances, and more. The Acts of the Apostles are really the Acts of the Spirit.

How does the Spirit's leading jibe with the way we do church to-day?

Committees, committees, committees: Adventists love committees. Are we committeed to death? Are we still flexible and open to present truth?

Let's step back and take a quick look at key moments in our history. Each was a *kairos*, a moment pregnant with promise. In focusing on the conferences that follow, I am aware that others might have been included—in particular, the 1901 General Conference Session.

Kairos Moments

Minneapolis, 1888: This conference was not held primarily to discuss theological matters—it was a General Conference Session, a business meeting. However, theological concerns quickly came to the fore, as Ellet J. Waggoner presented a series of Bible studies dealing with the Book of Galatians.

Waggoner's presentation focused on the "law" in Galatians. He argued that Paul meant law in general—both the Ten Commandments and the ceremonial law—and not just the latter, as stalwarts like Uriah Smith (*Review and Herald* editor) and George I. Butler (General Conference president) held.

Back of the specific issue was something far more important—soteriology. Are we saved by faith in Christ alone, or does salvation require obedience to the Ten Commandments, including the Sabbath?

Waggoner argued for the classic Reformation position of grace alone. In this he was supported by another young minister, Alonzo T. Jones. Both were bitterly opposed by the "leading brethren"—except for one person. Ellen White planted her flag with that of the Young

Turks—to her hurt. She witnessed her counsels come under attack and rejection. Later she would describe Minneapolis as the most painful episode of her long ministry.

New light was dawning, but most of those present couldn't see it. In the years following 1888, however, the gospel message proclaimed by Waggoner and Jones—boosted by Ellen White's preaching and writing—gradually won the day. Their message today is established Adventist doctrine, stipulated in the Fundamental Beliefs, although here and there contrary voices are still raised.

The 1919 Bible Conference: Chaired by General Conference President A. G. Daniells, the conference focused on the prophetic gift manifested in the Adventist Church. It candidly discussed questions that vex us to this day: the nature of Ellen's inspiration, literary borrowing, discrepancies, errors, and so on.

Here was present truth for Adventists in 1919. Many believers had embraced a faulty understanding of Ellen's inspiration: they tended to a verbal inspiration—every word dictated—view. Such a position was contradicted by the evidence of her own statements about the nature of inspiration and the evidence of how she worked described by those who had observed her closely.

Church members needed the "light" shed by the 1919 Bible Conference. They didn't get it. The material discussed at the conference was considered too "hot" for the people to handle, so it was put aside. Buried.

After many years a chance discovery of the minutes of the 1919 Bible Conference in the General Conference Archives brought the long-forgotten conference to light.

Glacier View, 1980: "Glacier View" has become a byword among Seventh-day Adventists. What happened or didn't happen, its meaning—the answers are legion.

Desmond Ford, a charismatic Adventist minister of exceptional intellect and powerful delivery, had fallen foul of retired ministers in Australia where he taught at Avondale College. The "brethren" arranged a transfer to Pacific Union College. Here, however, Ford's difficulties only increased, coming to a head in a Sabbath afternoon meeting on campus when he raised a series of questions centering on the church teaching of the heavenly sanctuary and prophecy. The meeting was recorded; tapes of it went viral.

The president of the church at that time, Elder Neal C. Wilson, a quintessential problem-solver (he never met a problem, small or big, that he could resist), decided to call an international theological conference to take up the issues raised by Ford.

It was a large group, some 116 in all: administrators, pastors, theologians. The five days together featured high hopes, frustration and disappointment, passion and promise. So many images still live starkly in my memory!

- Dr. Ted Heppenstall, Des' mentor, now aged, publicly pleading with Des to beware of making shipwreck;
- Elder Wilson's long appeal to Des before the assembled delegates, urging him to put his ideas "in his pocket" until the church saw light in them—only to have Des brusquely turn him down;
- Dr. Jack Provonsha on his feet, attempting to broker a public reconciliation between Des and the leaders from Australasia;
- Tough speeches from the South Pacific delegates and others calling Des to account.

Three of us from the Seminary—Fritz Guy, Gerhard Hasel, and I—had been appointed to draft a statement based on the daily discussions of the delegates. It was presented and discussed on Friday morning, then voted with strong support.

Dr. Ford announced that he could vote for the consensus statement.

Then, a surprise development: a new document was distributed, the authors unidentified. It pointed out areas where, it alleged, Ford was out of step with the church. This document was neither discussed nor put to a vote, but following the conference it rose to the fore. The consensus statement was quietly shunted aside.

So many years later, I remain troubled by the events of that Friday at Glacier View.

So what about Glacier View?

Was it a huge miscalculation on the part of the quintessential problem-solver?

A waste, a stacking of the deck?

A turning from our heritage of "present truth"?

Beware quick answers! In many respects Ford was his own worst enemy. Convinced that he was right, he was hard to help.

The International Prophetic Guidance Workshop, 1982: This event brought leaders and scholars together at General Conference headquarters to take up issues concerning Ellen White and her writings. Some of the issues were of long standing; others had been brought to light by Walter Ray in his explosive volume, *The White Lie.*

Attendees discussed 72 items ranging over the gamut of Ellen White studies. The papers were transparently open, frank, penetrating. Perhaps the most sensitive one came from Robert Olson, secretary (now called "director") of the White Estate, on "mistakes" in inspired writings. It began thus: "Are there discrepancies in the Holy Scriptures? The answer is, yes." He listed six categories of inaccuracy.

Olson then focused attention on the Ellen G. White corpus: "Turning now to the writings of Ellen G. White, we ask, are there discrepancies in her letters, articles and books? The answer is, Yes."

Delegates took home a large amount of printed material, 941 pages in all, and were encouraged to share it. The whole event, in my judgment, was a demonstration of present truth in action.

It was planned to hold similar conferences every five years or so. Alas, that didn't happen. This was the first and the last.

In some respects it was *déjà vu*—1919 over again. The discussions of the conference didn't get much coverage in the official press. Back in Australia, Dr. Arthur Patrick, director of the Ellen White Center, wrote two articles about the conference, but they were put on ice at the direction of the officers of the Australasian Division.

The Faith and Science Conferences, 2004: General Conference President Jan Paulsen decided on a bold initiative: a conference of theologians and scientists to take up issues of Creation and evolution. To guide the fraught endeavor, Paulsen turned to Elder Lowell Cooper, his most capable lieutenant and possibly the only Adventist who could bring the enterprise to a satisfactory finale.

The plan was to have each division of the world church conduct a mini-conference, with a final, global conference in Denver, Colorado. I was a delegate to this last, major conference.

I am not sure what Paulsen hoped to accomplish by all this effort. Perhaps to awaken an awareness of issues? To build understanding and trust? Whatever, his plan was in line with the Adventist heritage of openness to present truth.

The conference left me with mixed feelings. The presentations were honest and candid, and Cooper chaired the proceedings even-handedly. But the condescending attitude exhibited by some toward the scientists and the evidence they presented troubled me.

At the end of it all, the conference affirmed the Creation article in our Fundamental Beliefs—the only realistic outcome possible.

Have Our Doctrines Changed?

Yes, in ways that most of us can scarcely imagine.

The most fundamental of all fundamental beliefs is the doctrine of God. Here Adventist thinking has undergone profound change. James White and other pioneers didn't believe in the Trinity; in fact, they were anti-Trinitarian.

Likewise with the Son, the second Person of the Godhead: probably the majority of early Adventists held that the Son was an exalted being but created at a point in time. The Son was not eternally self-existent, one with God.

Ellen White's writings played a big role in helping to correct those ideas. Although in her earlier writings she described the Son in terms that could lead the reader to believe that her view was similar to her husband's, eventually she came out with categorical statements conforming to orthodox understanding, such as: "In Him [Christ] was life, original, unborrowed, underived" (*The Signs of the Times,* February 13, 1912).

Likewise with the Trinity doctrine: Mrs. White never used the term "Trinity," but in her later work she penned descriptions of the Godhead that taught that Father, Son, and Holy Spirit are co-equal and eternal.

During the 19th century, the masthead of the church's flagship paper, *The Review and Herald,* carried a simple statement of beliefs: "The commandments of God and the faith of Jesus." At that point in our history, doctrine and organization had the same stamp—simplicity. Just as the pioneers were leery of organization, so were they dead scared of any listing of doctrine that might in time become a creed.

Longtime *Review* editor Uriah Smith occasionally printed lists of doctrine, simply for descriptive purposes. One of these lists featured more than 30 items, several of which referred to areas of prophetic interpretation.

Nineteenth-century Adventism was a feisty fellowship wherein doctrinal matters and differences were openly discussed in the *Review*. Occasionally, however, ideas in vogue led some of the saints to question whether new ideas were bringing a departure from the basic message.

To such complaints Ellen White had a sharp rejoinder. What is all this talk about forsaking the pillars (sometimes called landmarks) of the faith? she wanted to know. To her there were only five pillars or landmarks: the Second Coming, the Sanctuary, the Sabbath, the State of the Dead, and the Spirit of Prophecy.

What about the five pillars today? All but one have undergone significant change since Ellen White's time.

The Second Coming: Our pioneers expected Jesus to return imminently. Time for them was very short, too short to plan long term. But the years passed; they still pass. Still we wait.

Inevitably, the relentless passage of the years called for adjustments in attitudes and thinking. Ellen White counseled Adventists on how to occupy the waiting time: not to teach that the Lord would come within five years, but not to put off His coming for 20 years. And to build—not temporary structures, but build well, build to last.

The Sanctuary: The pioneers pictured the heavenly sanctuary in literal terms that made the heavenly a glorified image of the earthly. Today, Adventists emphasize function rather than furniture, with

Christ's sacrifice and ministry taking pre-eminent place. And the teaching of the Investigative Judgment has morphed from anxiety to assurance.

The Sabbath: For 19th-century Adventists, the Sabbath teaching played a critical role. They believed that it was indispensible to salvation. No doubt some Adventists continue to hold a similar view. For others, however, the Sabbath is understood and observed within the orbit of grace. The thinking has shifted from demand to gift, from obedience to grateful response.

The Spirit of Prophecy: The Ellen G. White Board of Trustees for the past 30 years has pursued the goal of progressively releasing all the materials relating to Ellen White and her work. Today the vault is open to all researchers; nothing is off limits. In doing so the White Estate has been true to our heritage of present truth. Ellen White and her work have become the focus of historians of American church history, with major studies appearing, such as *Ellen Harmon White: American Prophet* (Terrie Dopp Hamodt, Gary Land, and Ronald E. Numbers, eds., Oxford, 2014).

The State of the Dead: Of the five pillars specified by Ellen White, this alone is unchanged from the time of the pioneers.

Adventists not so long ago commonly referred to their church as "the truth." In fact, however, it was a changing "truth," better described as "present truth."

The State of "Present Truth" Today

Are we still a people of present truth?

Yes, and no.

In several respects, theological thinking parallels our organization—bureaucratic, resistant to change, defensive. But the picture is mixed; there are many bits of evidence for the contrary side, evidences that present truth is not just a relic from the pioneers.

- Adventist scholars of Scripture now find a place alongside those of the leading universities of America and Europe. We are known and recognized for careful, thorough study of the biblical text.
- Adventist publishers have broken new ground. The Seventh-day Adventist Bible Commentary set was a landmark; it represented a major contribution in the tradition of present truth. Instead of dogmatic interpretations, it presented the reader with various options. The Biblical Research Institute has published significant works, such as the 2-volume set on the Remnant as well as the *Seventh-day Adventist Bible Handbook* (volume 12 of the Commentary Series).

The free church press, notably *Spectrum* and *Adventist Today*, increasingly plays an important role in stimulating Adventist thinking, at a time when the official publications have tended to follow a safe, non-controversial track.

I would like to close the discussion on this note, but candor mandates that I mention another side. A pall of suspicion has fallen over many of our theologians and scientists. The church in North America has become polarized, with the result that many of our finest scholars are excluded from contributing to the official publications of the church.

An example: When the SDA Bible Commentary was published in the 1950s, the Review and Herald, at that time rich and increased with goods, bore all the expense. Under the general editorship of Frances D. Nichol, the house co-opted the finest scholars in the church. Today, a totally new Bible Commentary is in the works. It will be published by Pacific Press (the Review and Herald, alas, is no more), but part of the funding will come from private sources. Remember the old line "He who pays the piper calls the tune?" This new, major work has fine scholars preparing the text, but it will not benefit from the contributions of some excellent scholars who have been deemed "unsafe" to be part of the project or who felt unable to conform to the stipulations laid down for writers.

That is sad.

The Wind Is Blowing

At times our lives seem "hard and dry," as the old hymn puts it. At times our beloved church seems to have lost is moorings, to have become a cage of suspicion, fault-finding, judgmentalism.

Take heart, dear friend. The big picture, the picture that God sees, is bright.

Is the Adventist cup half full or half empty?

For me, the answer is unequivocal: the Adventist cup is half full.

Yes, a lot of our churches feel like death. They are cold as the grave.

But! A lot of others are bursting with life. Centers of hope. Centers of healing. Centers of joy. Centers of energy.

New congregations are springing up. God is doing a "new thing," as He promises in His Word.

Centers where the Spirit is palpably present because Jesus is preached, Jesus is exalted as All—like The One Project.

The office of the Holy Spirit is to exalt Jesus. Not to lead us into some new religion, but back to the old, old story—Jesus and His love. When Jesus is acclaimed and permitted to be All, the Holy Spirit descends in power.

This is life.

This is movement.

This is present truth.

And it is happening, it is happening.

The wind is blowing. Do you hear it? Do you feel it?

CHAPTER SEVEN

The Other Elephant

As Jesus started on his way, a man ran up to him and fell on his knees before him. "Good teacher," he asked, "what must I do to inherit eternal life?"

"Why do you call me good?" Jesus answered. "No one is good—except God alone. You know the commandments: 'You shall not murder, you shall not commit adultery, you shall not steal, you shall not give false testimony, you shall not defraud, honor your father and mother.'"

"Teacher," he declared, "all these I have kept since I was a boy."

Jesus looked at him and loved him. "One thing you lack," he said. "Go, sell everything you have and give to the poor, and you will have treasure in heaven. Then come, follow me."

At this the man's face fell. He went away sad, because he had great wealth (Mark 10:17-22, NIV [cf. Luke 18:18-25; Matthew 19:16-22]).

This chapter will be, I fear, the most difficult writing I have ever attempted. Gladly would I leave it out of this book. But if I call the Adventist Church to honesty—as I do—I also must be honest.

Brutally honest.

Painfully honest.

Vulnerable.

I became acutely aware of the other elephant in the room in 2017, a few months after my book *Where Are We Headed?* hit the fan. That book brought a rash of speaking requests, usually several meetings spread over Friday evening and Sabbath. The first big one came from La Sierra University president Dr. Randall Wisbey. He thought that topics from the book might be helpful for the university's discussion at their annual Board of Trustees retreat.

A colleague teamed with me for informal discussions that filled sessions on Friday evening, Sabbath morning, and Sabbath afternoon. We simply drew up two chairs and dialogued close to the people, inviting them to participate.

And they did—with gusto!

From the opening remarks when we introduced ourselves, we made ourselves vulnerable. We spoke about our lives, spouses, children. We especially dwelt on the kids, our kids. With sadness we shared our hearts: our kids no longer value the Seventh-day Adventist Church as we do.

For me, it was a first. Like other Adventist preachers and teachers I'd often lamented the grim fact that Adventism is losing many of its best and brightest.

I'd said this, written this. It hurt, but not too badly.

When I came right out and said publicly that our kids, my kids, were part of the exodus from the church—that was a different matter. Saying it, sharing it, uncovered deep wells of pain.

Our honest, public sharing that Friday evening seemed to release a fountain of emotion. Person after person bared their heart with us. After the meeting was over some stopped by to let us know that we weren't alone in our pain: they too had sons or daughters who had left the church, some abandoning faith altogether.

The entire retreat brought wonderful, rich experiences and sharing. Noelene and I felt blessed, grateful to the Lord. It was that Friday evening together, when we opened our hearts to the group, that made the retreat so memorable.

All of us had come face to face with the second elephant—the departure of our children from Adventism.

Not our youth "leaving the church."

But my kids leaving the church.

It's the second elephant.

The first elephant is racism. It embarrasses us to talk about it.

The second elephant involves our kids. It hurts too much to talk about it.

What Happened?

How many times have I asked myself that question? How many times in the wee hours in my bed has my mind run back over the years and tried to figure it all out: What happened?

Unless I misread the state of Adventism in North America, a lot of you reading this chapter have asked or are asking with me: What happened?

I know for a fact that for many of you the deepest wish of your heart is that your daughter or son, when they come for a visit at Thanksgiving or Christmas, would go with you to church. Just to have them sitting alongside you like they used to, taking part in worship again—how your heart longs for that to happen.

Noelene and I have talked and prayed and thought a lot—a whole lot—about this matter. I'll briefly share some of our journey.

God blessed us with two wonderful children: a boy, then a girl. They are still wonderful. We love them and are proud of them—proud of their success in life (both have excelled in the marketplace) and proud of them in themselves.

We had a happy family. Not a lot of money, but fun. Love. Joy. Shared vacations.

Some people may have thought we had a model family. Although neither of us had formal training in child rearing, we were asked to present a series of talks on how to have a Christian family.

Back then, if anyone had suggested that the time would come when our kids no longer felt a connection with Adventism, I'd have said: "No way! Impossible!"

Noelene and I loved—still love—this church. I used to preach a sermon built on King David's heartbroken cry: "Oh, my son Absalom! My son, my son Absalom!" (2 Samuel 18:33). The title of my sermon was "A Father's Failure." I'd tell the people that no matter what I achieved in life, if my kids didn't stay with the church, I'd have been a failure.

Our son and daughter had all their education in Adventist schools right through the baccalaureate degree. They went to graduate studies in fine universities, and emerged still attending church, still Adventist. They entered the workplace as young professionals. They still went to church.

Gradually, however, something happened. Church attendance became less frequent. Often they couldn't find a compelling reason to get up on Sabbath morning. And when you don't attend, you get on a different path that slowly, but surely, leads away from the church.

They lived far from us. We didn't realize what was going on. By the time Noelene and I woke up, they'd crossed an invisible line and joined the majority of their peers—inactive or former Adventists. Christians, but not Seventh-day Adventist Christians; clean living with Adventist values, but not attached to the church.

It hurt me terribly. For a long time I didn't want to face up to what had happened. Noelene, more realistic than I, came to terms with the change faster than I did.

I used to lie awake nights rehashing the years, silently weeping over my failings as a father. With stabs of guilt and regret, I'd recall the many occasions on which I had put my work ahead of the family. One time kept coming back to haunt me. A high-powered committee of which I was a member was scheduled to convene at Newbold College in England. Our son, working in Germany, decided to come join me for the weekend so we could spend some time together.

We assumed that the committee would call a break for the Sabbath. Guess what? It did not. (Why do we—we leaders of the church—keep doing this? Don't we know that to keep the Sabbath—the *Shabbat*—means to rest? That's what the word means: a ceasing. Why don't we cease?)

I was torn. I wanted to be with my son. My heart told me I *ought* to be with him. But like the proper churchman that I was, I stayed with the committee. All day I tried to focus on the agenda items, but my mind was elsewhere.

Saturday night we got together at a restaurant. Sunday morning he boarded an airplane and flew back to Germany. I went to another session of the committee.

Working for the church brings special temptations. So easy to think that *we* are extra important in God's plan, that our *work* takes priority over everything else.

Our son never brought up that lost weekend. I know he was disappointed; I let him down. I couldn't spare time for him even on the Sabbath!

I've long since apologized. Some things, however, can never be made right. Opportunities that we let pass are gone forever. We can't bring them back.

A father's failure?

You'd better believe it!

Chances are that many of you reading these words identify with me in sorrow and regret. So let me take you beyond the past and share how I (and Noelene) have come to terms with our kids' leaving the Adventist Church.

Going Beyond Regret

We've come to realize that we aren't alone in this matter. Far from it: we are part of the majority.

I write with reference to Adventism in the developed world—America, Europe, Australia, and New Zealand. In other areas the picture may be more encouraging—for instance, in South America. I recall with delight an extended visit that Noelene and I made to the countries that form that great part of the world church. Everywhere we went, especially in Brazil, young men and women packed the churches, were taking the lead. Their joy and enthusiasm were infectious. We met a conference president who was only 28 years old. Some years after our visit, when division leaders selected a new president, they turned to the youth leader, Erton Kohler, who was 37.

On this trip, however, a senior leader uttered a disturbing caution. In a private conversation he shared this: "Here in South America, Adventists are proud that the church is growing much faster than in North America. But wait a few years and you'll find that it will become just like the situation you face."

Would to God time proves him wrong! This I know, however: in countries where Adventism has been established for more than a century—countries like Norway, Germany, Sweden, and France—the church is struggling to hold its own. It's on life support.

If we had been able to keep our young people in the fold, forget about evangelistic accessions, natural growth should have boosted our numbers far, far beyond what they are today.

Let's face it: *the Adventist Church in the developed world is unable to hold most of those who are born into it.* Young people go to church, attend Adventist schools, but eventually walk away.

Why?

Time to face facts. Time to acknowledge that Adventism has a *systemic* problem. We excel in bringing in new members (though public evangelism in the West has also fallen on hard times), but we fail to hold our own kids.

A cameo will make the point. When our son was in college, he formed a closely-knit friendship with six or seven other guys. They were a clean-cut, bright-eyed bunch of young Seventh-day Adventists. Their parents held "important" positions in the denomination— Seminary dean, professors, administrators. When they visited in our home, the young men exhibited a lively interest in the church and developments taking place within it. I thought it likely that several would place their considerable abilities to forwarding the mission of Adventism.

They did not. All went on to graduate school and then to hold down major positions in society. And all, with perhaps—I do not know—one or two exceptions, walked away from the Adventist Church.

Do we have a problem? You'd better believe it!

All my ministry I have felt a special concern for young people. If anything, my love and passion for them has only increased as my years mount up. You can't imagine the joy it brings me these days to have energetic, vibrant millennials invite me to speak at one of their gatherings, to be showered with love and respect, even though I now have to be helped onto the stage and remain seated as I speak.

What is going on? That question is with me day and night.

For years we've talked a lot of ballyhoo about our young people. The church of the future? No, the church of today. Putting the reins of leadership in their hands. Giving them a piece of the pie. Blah, blah, blah. Talk, talk, talk.

And they walk away.

We'd better start listening to them. Better start, earnestly, prayerfully, to try to figure out what's going on.

Nothing off limits.

No condescension.

No games.

Time, way past time, for open, honest, painful dialogue.

A friend who shares my passion put it this way: "If you want millennials to give you a hearing, they need to hear three things from you:

"First, will you accept everyone—*everyone*—without excluding anyone or any class of person?

"Second, will you let it be a two-way conversation? Will you listen as well as talk?

"Third, will you admit that you don't have all the answers, that you make mistakes? That you might be wrong?"

My friend concludes: "Unless you can talk to millennials on these three bases, you won't get anywhere."

A Voice From the Millennials

In November 2017, at the annual meeting of the Adventist Society of Religious Studies, six panelists presented written responses to my *Where Are We Headed?* The members of the panel were selected from different countries and levels of study.

Matthew Korpman, an undergraduate student at La Sierra University, wrote this about his fellow millennials:

> Dr. William Johnsson's work can be described as many things: timely, needed, powerful, controversial, straight-forward, Christ-centered, and even apocalyptic (it definitely reveals many things about us as a church). Its success lies in the fact that it truly gives voice and life to what I would call "the Adventist question."
>
> Johnsson's title, 'Where Are We Headed?' informs us less of a fact (where he believes we are) than it raises us to the awareness of a need to stop and reassess where we are, and more importantly, where we are going (something we as Adventist have often taken for granted). Likewise, his title evokes a double meaning, a more worrisome one, for it questions whether we are going somewhere spiritually (in the ultimate sense) that we may not wish to. It forces us to discover who it is that is guiding us to the direction we are going. Who is truly at the helm of our ship? The Spirit? Which? Like any good

question, Johnsson's work opens up more questions than it provides possible answers to. Those questions are needed now.

What is at stake in this question of Johnsson's is nothing less than the soul of the Church he, and all of us, so dearly care about. It's an issue that I care deeply about. Many are surprised to hear me, a Millennial, sounding passionate about a subject such as this. It's certainly not common. Johnsson's book touches on the Adventist Millennial problem a number of times. Don't most of my generation reject the church because of what they see happening within it, you wonder? Aren't Adventists losing hold on them quicker than sand slips though the fingers? The answer: Yes! We are. And that's exactly why Johnsson's work must be given ear.

Here's the diagnosis we don't want to accept: Millennials are not likely coming back any time soon (short of a miracle). There will not be a revival that we can plan that will accomplish this. The damage has been done: spiritually, theologically, and personally. We must learn and grow from this and only so that we have a potential chance to keep the ones we still have. That struggle is already one of our greatest.

Johnsson warns we are ready to lose the youth. He is most certainly correct. I know of countless Adventist Millennials, both those still in school *and those already employed in our church as ministers,* who speak openly with me that they are losing faith in serving our church. They are ready to quit or change denominations, especially since San Antonio's vote. Mind you: these are not disconnected youth who simply have stopped caring. These are deep thinking and faithful servants of Christ (the future of our church)! They are some of the brightest Adventists I've seen. They are our future, prophetic voices for our church who Christ is ready to use for His causes, those who could steer our Church in the right direction. Yet just when we are in need of these voices and the light they bring, that star is fading and doing so fast.

They see the Adventist Church as a patient dying in a hospital. This patient is not incurable, but the patient is obstinate, refusing to even acknowledge the true sickness it suffers from and thus, to accept the correct medication. They don't want to leave it, but they do not want to waste their time sharing its fate when there is a gospel to still be preached.

Is Adventism already dead? Some are asking this increasingly. I would argue no. It is however dead to many, even if not ultimately. Johnsson is reminding us in his work that there still is a future for this Church. It doesn't have to be this way. We can find our soul again. Yet, as he also wisely notes, "the Lord will not save us from ourselves." We have to make the choice. Will Christ be at the helm of our Advent ship (keeping the main thing the main thing) or will a new sense of papal power, like an iceberg, threaten any potential God might still have for us? Johnsson's work is a gift because it helps us to start this much needed conversation (truly commence it) so that the Holy Spirit may have a chance to lead us to answers that God would have us hear (*Spectrum*, November 27, 2017, vol. 45 no. 4, pp. 27-28).

Tough words! Church leaders, are you listening?

The Theological Knot

My mother's faith was staunchly practical. Rich in acts of kindness and goodness, the words of James 1:27 might have been her watchword: "Real religion, the kind that passes muster before God the Father, is this: Reach out to the homeless and loveless in their plight, and guard against corruption from the godless world" (MSG). Her ties to the Anglican church stretched back several generations.

Several years and several children into her marriage to my father, he joined the Seventh-day Adventist Church. For a while she struggled with faith questions but eventually decided to stay with the Church of England.

Eventually she bore 9 children; I came last. Among my siblings, the girls became Anglicans and the boys chose no religious affiliation. I, youngest of my mother's brood, decided to throw in my lot with Adventism.

She wasn't happy with the decision. I did not see her cry over it, but I suspect that all alone she shed tears. But she let me go because she loved me.

And shouldn't I let my children go, let them choose freely, because I love them?

We Adventists are strong advocates of religious liberty. We teach and believe that it's a God-given right, the most basic of human rights. We take our stand beside anyone whose religious freedom is endangered.

We must extend religious liberty to our own. In the past most Seventh-day Adventists believed that only they could be saved because they were the only Christians who obeyed the Ten Commandments—all of them, including the fourth, the Sabbath. No doubt many Adventists still hold this view, although it has never been part of our fundamental beliefs.

The teaching of righteousness by faith—that we are saved by grace alone, through faith alone in Christ alone—has steadily spread through the church, although not uniformly. Some areas of the world church retain the old, law-oriented understanding of salvation.

With grace becoming central in theology, the role of law, and the Sabbath in particular, has come to the fore. If there is nothing, *nothing,* we can do to add to the work of Jesus on the Cross, then Sabbath-keeping takes a new place. Whether we observe the Sabbath or not no longer determines our eternal standing with God.

Some Adventists, like those Christians in Paul's day who misunderstood his proclamation of the gospel to mean that the Lord no longer looked for obedience, have thrown out the Sabbath. Paul firmly rebuked those of his day with a stern "God forbid!" (Romans 3:31), and Adventists today who fall into a similar error make the mistake of throwing out the proverbial baby with the bathwater.

But practice tends to lag behind theology. I can affirm with my mind that a person doesn't have to be or remain an Adventist to be saved, but in my heart I fear for my child's eternal salvation when he or she quits the church.

In thinking like this I fall into an idea that the Scriptures do not teach. It arose in the second century and became entrenched, as it is still today in the Roman Catholic Church: *no salvation outside the church.*

For Christians in the Middle Ages, this teaching had immediate and practical implications. If the church disfellowships you, you no longer will have a priest to administer the last rites at the point of death, nor can you be buried in hallowed ground.

The Reformers broke sharply with this church-centered theology.

They emphasized the individual instead of the church, faith instead of dogma, grace instead of penance and pilgrimage.

As I think of the pain Noelene and I share with fellow church members whose kids no longer attend church, I have to ask myself: Have I fallen into the old way of thinking—a way that isn't biblical— of tying salvation to the Adventist Church instead of to Jesus Christ, who alone is the Way, the Truth, and the Life?

Jesus: it's all about Him. Without Him, church membership— membership in any church—counts for nothing. With Him at the center, church membership brings many blessings (fellowship, nurture, mission, to name a few).

So, dear friend, if your child loves Jesus but quits the Adventist Church, praise God that he or she knows the Lord. Salvation is all about Jesus.

Signs of Hope

In spite of the appalling losses of our sons and daughters, I am an optimist. I see signs of hope.

Again, let me remind you that I write with particular reference to Adventism in the developed world. Here and there churches are springing up that are drawing in millennials by the hundreds. It's happening in North America; it's happening in Australia; it's happening in South America.

I wondered if I'd ever see it: Millennials flocking into church on Sabbath morning. But I see it and rejoice.

One example among many: Crosswalk Church in Redlands, California. Come early or you won't find a seat. Three services every Sabbath. Church membership: about 900, but attendance is 1,500-2,000 (just the reverse of most churches). Tremendous energy. Warm fellowship. Strong involvement with the surrounding community. Average age of attendees: probably about 30.

These new churches point the way to a new Adventism. An Adventism that is *real*, that is down-to-earth, that is focused on Jesus. The preaching is biblical and powerful, the doctrine basic Adventist. A few aspects may shock you: the music is loud—make that *really* loud—and you may see a coffee bar (not Postum). Take a deep breath and open your heart. Feel the Spirit moving. Rejoice and celebrate with me.

This is Millennial Adventism. It's Adventism that works in 2018.

Once . . . Now

Once I was a proud theologian; I had all the answers.

Now I have only one answer.

Once I was a proud parent; I had all the answers.

Now I have only one answer.

But that answer is *the* Answer.

Jesus.

CHAPTER EIGHT

The Call of the Kingdom

When Jesus saw his ministry drawing huge crowds, he climbed a hillside. Those who were apprenticed to him, the committed, climbed with him. Arriving at a quiet place, he sat down and taught his climbing companions. This is what he said:

"You're blessed when you're at the end of your rope. With less of you there is more of God and his rule.

"You're blessed when you feel you've lost what is most dear to you. Only then can you be embraced by the One most dear to you.

"You're blessed when you're content with just who you are—no more, no less. That's the moment you find yourselves proud owners of everything that can't be bought.

"You're blessed when you've worked up a good appetite for God. He's food and drink in the best meal you'll ever eat.

"You're blessed when you care. At the moment of being 'care-full,' you find yourselves cared for.

"You're blessed when you get your inside world—your mind and heart—put right. Then you can see God in the outside world.

"You're blessed when you can show people how to cooperate instead of

compete or fight. That's when you discover who you really are, and your place in God's family.

"You're blessed when your commitment to God provokes persecution. The persecution drives you even deeper into God's kingdom.

"Not only that—count yourselves blessed every time people put you down or throw you out or speak lies about you to discredit me. What it means is that the truth is too close for comfort and they are uncomfortable. You can be glad when that happens—give a cheer, even!—for though they don't like it, I do! And all heaven applauds. And know that you are in good company. My prophets and witnesses have always gotten into this kind of trouble (Matthew 5:1-12).

Authentic Adventism hears the call of the Kingdom. Amid the din and clatter of modern life, the Kingdom calls. Calls us to values utterly different. To hopes and possibilities undreamed of. To the silence of eternity.

To the heart of God.

The call of the Kingdom comes to you and to me most clearly in the words of Jesus of Nazareth as He proclaimed His famous sermon on the hillside by the Lake of Galilee.

His words are the most often quoted but most unlived of all that He ever taught. From the day when they first fell from His lips to our times, people have marveled at their beauty, their simplicity, their profundity. And then gone away and lived in ways that deny them.

At his prayer meetings, Mahatma Gandhi liked to read from the Sermon on the Mount. Jesus' injunction not to resist evil with force but to turn the other cheek meshed with Gandhi's teaching and practice of *satyagraha*—truth force. Gandhi's use of non-violence as a political weapon befuddled the Brits and led to Indian independence.

But the new nation soon adopted a course at odds with Gandhi. Although he was honored and lauded by words and monuments, although his birthday, October 2, was made a national holiday, ere long India was developing nuclear weapons. The threat from China to the north and Pakistan to the west called for something beyond *satyagraha*.

Which raises the question: Did Jesus intend His words to be taken literally?

The Kingdom of Heaven

There is nothing in the Sermon on the Mount to suggest that Jesus was speaking in parables, as He often did elsewhere. To the contrary: He gives a series of examples that are all concrete—a dispute with someone who threatens to sue you, divorce, oaths, how to act when conscripted by the authorities, how to pray, how to fast, and so on.

But how to put His words in practice? That is the rub. What would happen if the president of the United States decided to apply Jesus' admonition to not resist evil? Wouldn't he or she be impeached for failing to fulfill the oath he/she took at the inauguration to uphold and protect the nation?

That hits the heart of the problem with Jesus' words. So beautiful, but impractical. So visionary, but hopelessly idealistic. Out of this world.

Some scholars have concluded that in the Sermon on the Mount Jesus proposed what they term an "interim ethic." They suggest that He expected to return to earth in a short while, so His followers would have to wait only a comparatively brief period. That is, the teachings in the Sermon were not intended to be an ongoing pattern for life in this world.

An interesting idea, but wrong. Throughout Matthew 5-7 we find not one mention of the Second Coming, last-day events, or an interim ethic. The tenor of the long passage runs in the opposite direction:

interpersonal relations with both friend and foe, concerns over food and clothing, acquiring wealth, and so on.

Recognizing this fact, most students of Scripture and many otherwise devout followers of Jesus of Nazareth feel satisfied to bracket off the Sermon on the Mount from instruction to be taken seriously in Christian living. They admire Jesus' words, but only in the same manner that they respect other notable passages in the scriptures of the world's religions.

All such approaches fall into a fundamental error: *Jesus' words are directed to citizens of the Kingdom of heaven, not to people in general.* They aren't intended to be a guide for government; far less do they provide a blueprint for handling the affairs of state. No, they speak directly and personally to each person who confesses Jesus as Savior and Lord.

Jesus' opening words show His intention: "You're blessed when you're at the end of your rope. With less of you there is more of God and his rule" (Matthew 5:3, MSG). He comes back to the idea in verses 19 and 20: "Trivialize even the smallest item in God's Law and you will only have trivialized yourself. But take it seriously, show the way for others, and you will find honor in the kingdom. Unless you do far better than the Pharisees in the matters of right living, you won't know the first thing about entering the kingdom." The "kingdom of heaven" is mentioned over and over in the Sermon on the Mount.

In the book of Matthew "kingdom of heaven" is a prominent expression; it occurs more than 50 times, sometimes as "kingdom of God." When John the Baptist began to preach, his message was: "Repent, for the kingdom of heaven has come near" (Matthew 3:2, NIV). That was the identical message of Jesus as He began His public ministry (Matthew 4:17).

For the large crowds who came out to hear John and later Jesus, the declaration that the Kingdom had drawn near must have produced a buzz of excitement. For centuries the Jews had prayed and looked forward to the time when God would intervene and liberate them from the yoke of the hated Romans. "The kingdom of God" would be the blessed time when the Anointed One, the Messiah, would appear. He would come in the spirit and power of Elijah and re-establish the glory of the monarchy to its status and power under King David.

Now, says John the Baptist, that time has drawn near. Now, says Jesus of Nazareth, it's here. *Now*!

See Jesus on the slope up from the Lake of Galilee. He has gathered about Him a band of followers, disciples, as did other rabbis of His time. But His words bring amazement, surprise, shock, hope, excitement. They are all about the Kingdom of heaven but in such a manner as to turn upside down the commonly held ideas of power, armies, liberation, and victory.

His very first words, "Blessed are the poor in spirit, for theirs is the kingdom of heaven" (Matthew 5:3, NIV), bewilder His hearers. No need to look ahead to battles, wars, and triumph over the enemies, because *the Kingdom of heaven is already here*. Some people are already in it.

That's shocking, bewildering, incomprehensible.

A second shock follows fast on its heels. Who are the people already in the Kingdom? Not some who've died and gone to heaven. Not generals, not freedom fighters.

None of these. Instead: the poor in spirit.

The Kingdom–NOW!

The Kingdom—not to the brave, not to the strong, not to the victor. But, to those who, in Eugene Peterson's words, "are at the end of their rope."

Weak.

Vulnerable.

Done for.

Whatever can Jesus mean? What sense can we today make of these strange words?

In *The Message*, Peterson's rendering of Jesus' words, we hear: "You're blessed when you're at the end of your rope. With less of you there is more of God and his rule."

I find fascinating this attempt to capture Jesus' meaning. Peterson, here as throughout *The Message*, abandons a strict, word-by-word translation of the biblical text in favor of taking its root ideas and expressing them in modern idioms. So here we find "God's rule" instead of the usual "kingdom of God." This interpretation isn't as divergent as it seems at first glance because the word translated "kingdom," the Greek *basilea*, can also mean "rule" or "reign." For Jesus' audience by the lake, however, they would surely have understood "the kingdom of God" in the traditional sense of liberation from bondage.

For us today, Peterson's "rule" instead of "kingdom" carries much more meaning. We have long since left behind the centuries when monarchs held sway, with the masses kept in subjugation. These are the days of democracy, elected officials, human rights, and the ballot box.

What then do Jesus' words convey to us? That wherever a person permits Jesus to be Lord of his or her life, the Kingdom of God is there. The day will come—the day of Jesus' Second Coming—when the Master will reign as King of Kings and Lord of Lords; then the Kingdom of God will appear in its ultimate manifestation. But we do not have to wait until then to find the Kingdom of God. The Kingdom is already here. The Kingdom is now!

Hear again Jesus' words: "Blessed are the poor in spirit, for theirs is the kingdom of heaven."

John the Baptist: the Kingdom is near.

Jesus: the Kingdom is here!

How Can it Be?

For Jewish critics of Jesus of Nazareth, the argument is simple: Jesus claimed to be bringing the Kingdom of God, but it did not happen. He was wrong. Jesus wasn't the Messiah, although He thought that He was.

Who was wrong—Jesus or His critics?

If you understand the Kingdom to mean power, force, and victory, the critics got it right.

But if you understand the Kingdom as Jesus set it out in the Sermon on the Mount—as a spiritual thing, the rule of God in the heart of individuals—Jesus was right. His Kingdom did break in to earth in His life and ministry. He changed the world, changed it irrevocably.

But how can it be? Does this talk about "kingdom" or "rule" make any sense? Look at Jesus' words in the Sermon: the poor in spirit, the mourners, the meek, the peacemakers, the persecuted. And later in the Sermon: turning the other cheek, cooperating with the Roman soldier who compels you to carry his armor, and so on.

What sort of "kingdom" is this? How can we even talk about "kingdom" or "rule?"

Not so fast!

Don't forget Mahatma Gandhi, the little old man in a loincloth who brought the mighty British Empire to its knees. His strategic approach to liberating his people—*satyagraha* (literally, "truth pressure")—derived from Jesus' call to non-violence in the Sermon on the Mount.

Don't forget Dr. Martin Luther King, Jr. In leading the struggle for dignity and civil rights for African Americans, King took his cue from Gandhi. Like Gandhi's followers in India, those who joined King were beaten and abused, kicked and clubbed, spat upon, trampled, jailed. Some paid the ultimate price: they died in the conflict.

Like Gandhi and his followers, they renounced the use of force. When bashed and beaten, they did not resist. They simply bore the blows, the insults, the injustices. They did not retaliate.

The day came when the Brits packed up and left India, the jewel in the crown of empire. They simply gave up; a power greater than guns and tanks had won the day. *Satyagraha* had triumphed.

And the non-violent campaign of Dr. King also won the day in the United States. White consciences became aroused as television flashed images of water cannons mowing down unarmed men and women, of savage dogs unleashed on helpless bodies. It became too much to bear. Something had to change.

Change came in the form of legislation enacted by Congress. Segregated restaurants, segregated restrooms, segregated schools—all were swept away. The quintessential American right—the right to vote—at last was extended to the country's citizens who happened to be born with a black skin.

Jesus—Gandhi—King.

The Sermon on the Mount doesn't make people weaklings. Jesus didn't call His followers—those who heed the call of the Kingdom—to be doormats.

Another example, as current as today. I turn on the television and watch in wonder as David Letterman interviews Malala Yousafzai.

What a contrast—the short young woman in a headscarf alongside this tall older man with a long, white beard. He towers over her.

But a funny thing happens as the interview rambles forward: before my eyes the 19-year-old slip of a girl grows taller and taller. She looks Letterman straight in the eye, no hint of nervousness or apprehension. Some of Letterman's off-the-wall questions puzzle her, but she displays not one second of fear. Her answers come fast, unrehearsed, direct, wise, powerful.

Answers from a young woman who has looked death in the eye, whose work puts her at continual risk of another bullet to her head.

This young girl amazes me. I feel like jumping up and applauding as she shares a passion for the education of girls everywhere, for deliverance of girls from child marriages, for equality and opportunity for all God's daughters.

Malala is a giant, a wonderful human being. The Nobel committee made a superb choice when they selected her at age 17 to receive the most coveted award, the Peace Prize.

I was transfixed by the interview, the program of the Incredible Woman Giant and the Incredible Shrinking Host. It was all so rich, so encouraging, so inspiring. For me, its peak came near the end when Letterman asked Malala how she feels about the young man whose bullet had almost ended her life. Speaking quietly, she said that she forgave him, "because revenge can never bring healing to this world's wounds."

I have no knowledge of how Malala relates to Jesus of Nazareth. But whether she's a professed Christian or not, the remarkable witness of her life and words bear the stamp of Jesus' famous sermon by the lake.

It's time now to look at a little history, to see developments that transmogrified early Christianity. This consideration will call attention to a player in world history whose name has a familiar ring for Seventh-day Adventists—the Roman emperor Constantine (280s-337 AD).

The Man Who Stole the Kingdom

Constantine the Great, who ruled over the Roman Empire from 306 to 337, is revered as a saint in both the Roman Catholic and Greek Orthodox traditions. He was the first emperor to embrace Christianity, although he waited until he was on his deathbed to be baptized.

Seventh-day Adventists have a much more problematic view of Constantine. They attribute to him a key role in the change of the day of worship from the biblical Sabbath to Sunday, "the venerable day of the sun."

But Constantine's negative influence on Christianity stretched far beyond the Sabbath-Sunday concern. With him began a deadly union of the state with the church: Christendom.

Constantine had been a worshiper of the "Unconquered Sun," whom he regarded as his patron deity. But in 312 he experienced a dramatic change of religion. At this time he was competing with Maxentius for mastery of the western empire. Before Constantine marched into Italy against Maxentius, he saw a vision of the cross in the sky. The night before he met Maxentius in battle (at the Milvian Bridge), he had a dream in which he was commanded to mark his soldiers' shields with the monogram of Christ—formed of the two initial letters of the Greek name of Christ: X (ch) and P (r).

Constantine defeated Maxentius; the battle was decisive. From that time Constantine considered himself to be in a special sense under the guidance of the God of Christianity. He adopted the XP monogram combined with the cross as his *labarum*—the standard that went before him into battle.

What a departure from the words and example of Jesus, who refused to call down legions of angels when He was arrested, and who warned, "All who use swords are destroyed by swords" (Matthew 26:52, MSG)! Now Christianity itself—the religion of the Sermon on the Mount—was enlisted to justify warfare.

This development in the church led to a radical transformation of its character. It didn't merely change; it was transmogrified. As the papacy grew in strength and influence, the church increasingly merged with the state. The head of Christianity became in effect a sovereign who took his place alongside the other monarchs of Europe. Except that the Pope was more than a temporal king: he claimed to wield influence not only for this life but for events beyond this world.

With Augustine (354-430) the transformation of Christianity was completed. This theologian of towering intellect, in his classic *The City of God,* argued that the "kingdom of heaven" proclaimed by Jesus was meant to be realized on earth. As the church extended its power and reach ever further, the Kingdom would come on this earth. No need for the Second Coming: the church would make it happen.

The church did indeed grow in power and influence, but in ways that made a mockery of the Sermon on the Mount. While popes and prelates lived in luxury, the common people, for whom the Scriptures were forbidden, groped after God in fear, ignorance, and superstition.

By the time of Martin Luther and the other Reformers, the corruption and venality of the Church had sunk so low that something had to give. And give it did: the Reformation exploded on Europe like a bomb.

Luther, Calvin, Knox, Zwingli brought many reforms, but their efforts fell short of returning Christianity to its first-century teachings. Except for the Anabaptists, the idea of church allied with the state persisted. Luther's reforms depended on the protection of the princes who ruled over states in Germany. The idea of a church without state tutelage was foreign to him.

Thus, we find Luther employing the ugliest, most vehement language in support of the state when the peasants revolted. "Kill, Maim! Murder!" His language is so violent, so outrageous by our norms that it makes your hair stand on end.

How could the great reformer, lauded by Ellen White in *The Great Controversy* and a hero in Adventist lore, take such a position? Because of the idea of Christendom—a Christian nation—that stems from Constantine.

For many years I loved the hymn "Onward, Christian Soldiers." It has a rollicking tune; I sang it with gusto.

No more. Today I cannot bring myself to say the words: "marching as to war/ with the cross of Jesus going on before."

That idea, if not the words, was employed in the slaughter of men, women, and children. Urged on by the Pope, the Crusaders set out to reclaim the Holy Land from the hands of the Muslims. They marched under the banner of the cross, literally—"with the cross of Jesus going on before"— on marauding campaigns of blood, murder, rape, and pillage.

Onward, Christian soldiers? Today, knowing what I know, the words repulse me. I wish Adventists would be educated in its history and banish the hymn from their worship services.

It's time to get back to Jesus.

Time to get back to the Sermon on the Mount.

Time to be authentic Christians. Authentic Adventists.

Adventists and the Sermon on the Mount

Kindly indulge me in a story.

It goes way, way back. I am 18 years old and the Korean War is raging. In Australia the government introduces "national service," a program similar to the draft in the United States. Every male who turns 18 has to be registered and report for 98 days of basic training.

I am a new Christian: a couple of years back I fell in love with Jesus of Nazareth and was baptized. And I am a new Seventh-day Adventist: I have studied their teachings and concluded that, among the many denominations that claim to follow Jesus, this is the one whose beliefs are closest to those of the New Testament church.

In this time of conscription, Adventists hold a teaching that stands out from the crowd: they advocate non-combatancy. As a recent convert to the faith, I adopt this stance. But unlike the situation in America, I can't get this status simply by applying for it. I have to appear before a magistrate and argue my case. No one is permitted to speak on my behalf.

As I stand in the dock before the magistrate, the state puts up a prosecutor who peppers me with questions that test my sincerity. He opens a Bible and quotes: "He teaches my hands to war." It's a tough experience, but the magistrate eventually grants me non-combatant status.

The evening newspaper carries a story on the proceedings.

And so, to boot camp. I drill with the other soldiers but don't carry a rifle. Platoon sergeant Gloyne tells me: "Johnsson, if it's the last thing I do, I'll see you carrying a gun!"

After several weeks everyone in the camp assembles on the parade ground for inspection by the commanding officer. One soldier of the hundreds on the parade ground isn't carrying a weapon. The

CO calls for a sergeant to get me out of there.

After that my daily routine changes: I no longer march with the others; I'm assigned to the officer's mess hall for menial duties, later to the camp hospital to work as an orderly.

At last the lonely ordeal comes to a close and I go home.

As a teenager I was shy, bookish. I hated the military. Saturdays at camp I'd head for the bush with my Bible and Sabbath school quarterly. Sunday mornings the other guys marched to "church parade," but I had to work doing odd jobs in the camp store.

I had the earnestness of the convert, the zeal of the true believer.

Adventist young men in other countries went through much more for their non-combatant convictions. Some went to jail; some were beaten; some gave their lives.

Like them, I felt I was following in the footsteps of Jesus who, by word and life, eschewed violence. I still hold these convictions.

It perplexes me, therefore, to observe that American Adventism has largely abandoned non-combatancy, a stance that came down to us from the pioneers of the movement. Today many thousands of Adventist men and women serve in the United States military. They do so by choice; there is no draft.

I don't question the actions of these young people. No doubt for many the military provides opportunities to better themselves through education and training. I salute their courage and devotion to country. To fight or not to fight, to bear arms or to be non-combatant: it is an individual decision that I respect.

But this change from early Adventism—for change it is, and one that is not endorsed by the European Adventist Church—makes me wonder. Have we let go of the call of the Kingdom in other areas as well?

The kingdom (lower case) and the Kingdom (upper case)

The kingdom (society) says:

Blessed are the strong, the proud, the self-sufficient.

But the Kingdom calls:

Blessed are the vulnerable, the weak, for God can be their all-sufficiency.

The kingdom says:

Blessed are those who are "cool."

But the Kingdom calls:

Blessed are those who are broken, because they are ready for Jesus to rule their lives.

The kingdom says:

Blessed are the assertive.

But the Kingdom calls:

Blessed are those who know themselves, who are content with who they are.

The kingdom says:

Blessed are those who acquire the greatest number of life's toys.

But the Kingdom calls:

Blessed are those who desire Jesus more than anyone or anything.

The kingdom says:

Blessed are the tough.

But the Kingdom calls:

Blessed are the kind, the gentle, the thoughtful.

The kingdom says:

Blessed are those who look and act smart.

But the Kingdom calls:

Blessed are those whose inner life isn't in tension with the front they show to others.

The kingdom says:

Blessed are the forceful, the winners.

But the Kingdom calls:

Blessed are those who know that God is Father of all and we are one family.

The kingdom says:

Blessed are the people on top, who get by with lying and cheating.

But the Kingdom calls:

Blessed are those who love God and put Him first, no matter the cost.

CHAPTER NINE

His Love, Our Love

Just before the Passover Feast, Jesus knew that the time had come to leave this world to go to the Father. Having loved his dear companions, he continued to love them right to the end. It was suppertime. The Devil by now had Judas, son of Simon the Iscariot, firmly in his grip, all set for the betrayal.

Jesus knew that the Father had put him in complete charge of everything, that he came from God and was on his way back to God. So he got up from the supper table, set aside his robe, and put on an apron. Then he poured water into a basin and began to wash the feet of the disciples, drying them with his apron. When he got to Simon Peter, Peter said, "Master, you wash my feet?"

Jesus answered, "You don't understand now what I'm doing, but it will be clear enough to you later."

Peter persisted, "You're not going to wash my feet—ever!"

Jesus said, "If I don't wash you, you can't be part of what I'm doing."

"Master!" said Peter. "Not only my feet, then. Wash my hands! Wash my head!"

Jesus said, "If you've had a bath in the morning, you only need your

feet washed now and you're clean from head to toe. My concern, you un-
derstand, is holiness, not hygiene. So now you're clean. But not every one
of you." (He knew who was betraying him. That's why he said, "Not every
one of you.") After he had finished washing their feet, he took his robe, put
it back on, and went back to his place at the table.

Then he said, "Do you understand what I have done to you? You ad-
dress me as 'Teacher' and 'Master,' and rightly so. That is what I am. So
if I, the Master and Teacher, washed your feet, you must now wash each
other's feet. I've laid down a pattern for you. What I've done, you do. I'm
only pointing out the obvious. A servant is not ranked above his master; an
employee doesn't give orders to the employer. If you understand what I'm
telling you, act like it—and live a blessed life....

"Let me give you a new command: Love one another. In the same way
I loved you, you love one another. This is how everyone will recognize that
you are my disciples—when they see the love you have for each other" (John
13:1-17, 34-35).

So here we have it, from the lips of the Master Himself: "This is how everyone will recognize that you are my disciples—when they see the love you have for each other."

Not how much we *know*, but how much we *love*.

This is the criterion of genuine Christianity. This is the test of authentic Adventism.

This test embraces all that comes before in this book, all the other marks of the genuine over against the fake. It is the acid test.

I have to wonder: How come I hear so little about it in my church? More to the point, how come I have preached and written so little about it?

Over the years I have observed that we Adventists in general are reticent to speak about Jesus. This contrasts sharply with what I have noticed from Evangelical Christians. They speak spontaneously, unabashedly; we tend to be tight-lipped.

Why is this?

I confess to my own failings in this regard. Among Adventists I could speak freely about my Lord, although, as noted above, Adventists don't do this very much. But with others around, as in a restaurant, I didn't talk about Jesus. The church? No problem. Other friends? No problem. But my Best Friend? Silence.

I wonder how my Best Friend feels about this behavior.

I don't think my reticence in this regard was out of the ordinary. As I reflect on the sermons and articles of our leaders, how rarely do any share personally their love for Jesus. Lots about the church, quotations from Ellen White about Jesus—yes. But expressions of love for Jesus? Silence.

How different from Ellen White's practice! She expressed her love for Jesus unreservedly, personally, beautifully. Why can't we be more like her?

Noelene and I are sitting in a crowded restaurant in Sydney. The tables are laid out in close proximity with one another. Noelene and I have come to speak at meetings of the One Project. Sydney is a highly secular city. In the past I would have cringed inwardly if someone at out table had begun to talk openly about Jesus. People around us would think we were weird, religious nuts.

But Noelene and I are conversing openly about Jesus, without any attempt to lower our voices or to quickly change the subject. Our hosts, Rod and Zan Long, are vibrant Christians, Adventists who play major roles in the One Project meetings—Zan runs the children's meetings, while Rod takes care of visuals and audio.

I owe to wonderful people like Zan and Rod a change in my practice. After so many years I feel like the man whose tongue was loosed by Jesus and who began to speak freely.

For me the lesson is simple: when we focus on Jesus, we want to speak about Him without hesitation, no matter the situation in which we find ourselves.

All About Jesus

I plan to write about Jesus right here. But I feel grossly inadequate to take up the task. How to reduce the preciousness of Jesus—in His tender, loving care; His kindness; His compassion; His sweetness; His unfailing, steadfast mercy—to words on paper? He has always been there for me. He has always come through when I need Him most. He has never let me down, never upbraided me for my foolishness, my inconsistency.

His love is wonderful—wonderful to me. What more can I say.

Those who know *Him*—not just about Him, but *Him*—will understand. My words, feeble as they are, will resonate in their souls. For them as for me, Jesus is the Lily of the Valley, the Fairest Among Ten Thousand, the Bright and Morning Star.

Jesus is All.

All now and forever.

All.

He is love. In His love we find love. In His love our hearts stretch out to other hearts and embrace them. We join hearts with one another because the love of Jesus is at the center; we are knit together with Him and so with one another.

The pagans in the early centuries couldn't help noticing how different the followers of Jesus were. "How these Christians love each other!" they marveled.

It was as Jesus said it would be: by their love for one another the followers of Jesus bore a stamp, a sign, a mark of the love of the Risen Lord.

As I write these lines, my heart is still full to bursting with an experience from the very recent past. Lines from a source long forgotten keep coursing through my head:

"That though the heart

Should burst with more,

It could not live with less."

Noelene and I spent the weekend at a church retreat in the mountains of southeastern California. Perhaps 500 people were there—babes in arms, hordes of bright-eyed teens, young adults, all the way up to seniors with walkers. The two days, packed with powerful preaching, great music, delicious food, and fun, made for one of the most unforgettable experiences of our entire lives.

What made this retreat so incredibly rich with inspiration and fellowship? I think it was the way the organizer of the weekend opened the event. "Throughout this weekend," he requested, "let it be Jesus, Jesus, Jesus. Jesus in everything. Jesus all the time."

And it was. Jesus was All.

That made the difference. Focusing on Him and His love warmed our hearts, melted the ice between strangers, freed us up to laugh and rejoice.

Our love for Jesus is expressed best in song rather than theology:

"As the deer pants for the water, so my soul longs for you."

"He took me into His banqueting hall and his banner over me was Love."

"Christ alone, Cornerstone, weak made strong in the Savior's love."

So to John chapter 13. We will work through it in order, noting what it tells us about love—God's love.

The chapter begins with Jesus' love (verses 1-17) and closes with our love for one another (verses 34-35).

Jesus' Love

"Just before the Passover feast, Jesus knew that the time had come to leave this world and go to the Father. Having loved his dear companions, he continued to love them right to the end," John tells us.

The words translated as "right to the end" can be understood in a different sense in the original. "End" can have, instead of a *time* reference, the meaning of *degree*. The New International Version prefers the latter and translates it as: "he showed the *full extent* of his love."

I think this understanding of the Greek text is the correct one. John immediately follows with the account of Jesus washing the disciples' feet. John is telling us: see how great is Jesus' love. See the extent to which it takes Him—even to humbling Himself to perform the most menial of tasks!

Let's try to put ourselves in the picture. People wear sandals—no socks—and roads are unpaved. Inevitably your feet get dirty after only a short walk.

When you arrive at someone's home, the first item of business is to remove your sandals and wash your feet. After you wash, the water is brown—very different from the water after an Adventist foot-washing service.

The water not only cleans off the dust, it gives a nice, cool refreshing lift to your weary feet.

Slavery is common throughout the Roman Empire. The slaves perform a variety of duties, but washing the feet of guests isn't one of them. *But Jesus washes the disciples' feet!* Do you begin to get the picture? Jesus stoops to do what even the household slave isn't required to do.

Jesus got His hands dirty. And so must we if we claim to be His followers. We will serve people who aren't "nice," people who are broken, people who look bad and smell bad, people who are homeless, sick, behind bars. In serving them we serve Jesus (Matthew 25:31-46).

Oh, what a far cry from the manner in which so-called followers would conduct themselves in later centuries! Priests, prelates, and popes would live in luxury—building bishops' palaces, accumulating treasures of art and sculpture, calling down divine support for their authority, holding men and women hostage to fear of eternal retribution!

Jesus said: "Whoever wants to be great must become a servant. Whoever wants to be first among you must be your slave. That is what the Son of Man has done: He came to serve, not to be served—and then to give away his life in exchange for many who are held hostage" (Mark 10:43-45, MSG).

No appeal to authority, no parading of position.

This is what Jesus said.

This is what Jesus did.

Jesus washed their feet.

Adventists, are you listening?

After Jesus had removed the apron and sat down, He told the Twelve: "If I, the Master and Teacher, washed your feet, you must now wash each other's feet. I've laid down a pattern for you. What I've done, you do" (John 13:14-15, MSG).

Seventh-day Adventists are one of the very few churches that take Jesus' words literally. We practice ritual foot washing prior to the Communion service. It is a simple, beautiful act of love and humility, when tears of love often flow freely.

But look again at the story. There is more here than Jesus leaving us an example.

A Prophetic Sign

When Jesus comes to Peter with the basin, Peter remonstrates: "You're not going to wash my feet—ever!" Jesus replies: "If I don't wash you, you can't be part of what I'm doing." What did Jesus mean by these words?

The NRSV translates verse 8: "Unless I wash you, you have no share with me." Raymond Brown in his outstanding commentary on John, renders: "If I do not wash you, you will have no heritage with me."

Peter doesn't get it. "Master!" he exclaims. "Not only my feet, then. Wash my hands! Wash my head!"

Peter can only think about dirty feet, but Jesus has much more in mind. "One who has bathed does not need to wash, except for the feet," Jesus tells Peter, "but is entirely clean" (verse 10, NRSV). Eugene Peterson, in *The Message*, attempts to bring out Jesus' meaning by inserting words not in the original text: "My concern, you understand, is holiness, not hygiene."

What lies behind the cryptic words of Jesus in this scene? The clue to the answer lies, I think, in Jesus' response to Peter: "You don't understand now what I'm doing, but it will be clear enough to you later" (verse 7, MSG).

Not now—later!

And later, not much later, some 12 hours hence, Jesus will be impaled on a cross outside the city gate. Then He won't lay aside His robe; it will be stripped from him. All His garments will be taken until He is left naked to the sky, an object of shame and loathing.

Women who followed Him from Galilee will be there—standing at a discreet distance so as not to gaze on His nakedness.

The soldiers who executed Him parted His garments into four

piles and gambled for them, the beloved John records (John 19:23-25). Four parts—the long tunic (the *chiton*), the outer garment (the *humartia*), the headpiece or turban, and the loincloth. They took it all from Him, leaving Him exposed, naked, bare.

It was Roman "justice" on full display. Crucifixion, reserved for the worst offenders, was brutal—and public. Get the message: this is what you can expect if you have ideas of setting up yourself as a king! We will kill you in the worst manner imaginable. It will be a horrible, painful, shameful end with everybody looking on.

The writer to the Hebrews tells us that our Lord "endured the cross, disregarding its shame" (Hebrews 12:2, NRSV). He suffered the ultimate humiliation.

Yet it was more. That cross—that symbol of shame, of humiliation—became the instrument of our salvation.

Because of His dying, we live.

Through His humiliation, we are set free.

All this was foreshadowed in the act and words of Jesus on that Thursday night prior to the Crucifixion. What He did was a prophetic sign pointing the disciples to the momentous events soon to break upon them.

Humiliation before Ultimate Humiliation.

Washing before Ultimate Cleansing.

Our Love

From "Jesus love" John 13 takes us to our love:

"Let me give you a new command: Love one another. In the same way I loved you, you love one another. This is how everyone will recognize that you are my disciples—when they see the love you have for each other" (verses 34-35, MSG).

Twice more in Jesus' Farewell Discourse (John 14-17), He gives the same instruction: love one another (John 15:12, 17). "Love" in both noun and verb forms dominates these chapters—we find it occurring some 25 times. In all cases the Greek word used for "love" is *agape*, signifying the highest type of love, love that begins with God and flows to relations among the disciples of Jesus.

The beloved disciple John, who I think wrote the Fourth Gospel, late in life sent letters to the early Christians. Three of these letters have survived; we know them as 1, 2, and 3 John. One is clearly addressed to an individual, Gaius (3 John); another may be also (2 John). John calls himself "the elder." These epistles come late in his life.

An interesting vignette has come down to us from the church father Jerome. He recounts a tradition that the aged John always had the same message for followers of Jesus, one that could be reduced to, "My little children, love one another."

This message echoes through the three letters that we have in our Bible. We hear "love" as noun or verb more than 30 times in 1 John, where the entire fourth chapter can be understood as a meditation on Jesus' words found in John 13:34-35: "Let me give you a new command: Love one another. In the same way I loved you, you love one another. This is how everyone will recognize that you are my disciples—when they see the love you have for each other."

As the shadows of evening steadily lengthen in my life, I find myself increasingly drawn to the letters of the beloved disciple. I have spoken and written very little on these epistles, but at this stage of life they resonate with my experience in Christ. I should be delighted to be remembered as a follower of Jesus whose constant theme was "Little children, love one another."

But Jesus' call to love one another is couched in a setting that seems strange; it comes as a command. How can this be? Love is free-ly given; it cannot be commanded.

The New Command

In Leviticus 19:18 we read: "Love your neighbor as yourself. I am the Lord." Since the command to love is at least as old as Moses, how come Jesus could call it a *new* command?

The aged apostle gives us help:

"My dear friends," he says. "I'm not writing anything new here. This is the oldest commandment in the book, and you've known it from day one. It's always been implicit in the Message you've heard. On the other hand, perhaps it is new, freshly minted as it is in both Christ and you—the darkness on its way out and the True Light already blazing!" (1 John 2:7-8, MSG).

Jesus—He makes the difference. The love command is all about Him. It's in Jesus, only in Jesus, that we see what *agape* love is really like. Jesus didn't just command. He *demonstrated* it.

There's another difference between Moses' stipulation in Leviticus and Jesus' new commandment. Jesus is not talking about loving our neighbor, as Moses was; He's dealing with love among His follow-ers. True, He calls us to love our neighbors, getting our hands dirty for them. All true. But in the Farewell Discourse, love is all about Jesus and the disciples. The *agape* love that flows from God binds them together and is a wonder to the world.

With Jesus' words about His love and our love, we've gone way beyond a religion based on law and obedience. We're in new terri-tory, where the old norms no longer hold. We've passed from tables of stone to fleshy tables of the heart, from old covenant to new cov-enant, from checklist performance to something that can never be measured: love. Who can ever say that they have loved enough?

The old covenant had stipulations—the Ten Commandments. Those precepts, a transcript of God's character, will always abide. The new covenant has a new command, new in Jesus: "Love one another, as I have loved you."

Adventists and the Acid Test

How do we stack up? Do we pass the acid test—the love test?

Yes—and no.

On one hand, Adventists have great fellowship. I have benefited from that warm embrace; I love it. When I cut ties with family and friends and cast in my lot with the Adventists, I was welcomed, I was loved.

I still am.

I'm still grateful for that love.

But. . . .

Too often we put up barriers of our own construction, not of God's. We divide between "us" and "them." Yes, right in the Adventist fellowship.

We think of ourselves as an end-time people (Good). But too often we get sucked up in end-time conspiracy theories and paranoia that leave us suspicious and judgmental of our fellow believers. We deny Jesus' love commandment by our actions.

Along with this failing, we tend to be exclusive. We think and act as though we're the only people on earth that God is looking out for.

We're not.

He's a big, big God.

We need to read Jesus' heart-searching parable uttered just before He went to the Cross—Matthew 25:31-46. It will shake us out of our self-absorption and exclusivism.

Love That Drives Out Fear

There's way too much fear among Seventh-day Adventists:

- Pastors, teachers, leaders afraid to speak their mind for fear of losing their jobs,
- Kids taught "Oh, be careful little hands what you do.... Be careful little feet where you go.... Be careful little eyes what you see.... There's a Father up above," looking down to catch every slip,
- Youth scared to death of the Time of Trouble, Last Day Events, Catholic plots, death decrees, and more—eschatology run amok!
- Adults living all their lives in the church but who never "get it."

Once after I preached on the grace of Jesus (what else is there to preach on?), an old lady waited in the pews to see me. The conversation went like this:

"I'm 86. I was brought up Adventist. I attended Adventist schools. I've attended church all my life. But I never felt sure of my salvation; I didn't know if I was going to make it after all.

"Today, for the first time in my life, I know that Jesus will take me to be with Him forever. I'm no longer afraid of the future, no longer afraid of dying.

"Thank you!"

There's way too much fear among Seventh-day Adventists.

Any fear would be too much.

Over and over Jesus said, "Fear not!" to scared, apprehensive men and women.

He says today: "Fear not."

Writes the beloved John: "There is no room in love for fear. Well-formed love banishes fear. Since fear is crippling, a fearful life—fear of death, fear of judgment—is one not yet fully formed in love" (1 John 4:18, MSG).

Love and the Fundamental Beliefs

By now some readers of this book are wondering, What about doctrine—where does that fit in? What about the 28 Fundamental Beliefs?

Doctrine is important for us individually and as a church. Doctrine helps to define who we are: it shows where we are similar to other denominations and where we differ—what sets us apart from other Christians.

I hold the 28 Fundamental Beliefs in high regard. I had a part in formulating the 27 that were adopted at the 1980 General Conference Session, and then again in shaping the 28th, which was added at the 2005 Session. That responsibility—working on both the 27 and the 28th—says something about me: I value these statements.

Although some among us have tended to question the necessity of the 28, I have experienced their value in helping to separate our genuine teachings from others that may be put forward from time to time.

Years ago on the John Ankerberg Show, I faced a barrage of hostile questions on live TV. Host Ankerberg and guest Walter Martin came armed with an arsenal of embarrassing quotes they had gleaned from Adventist publications. To each example they brought up, my reply was: "Only the Fundamental Beliefs give the official understanding of doctrine. That idea an individual wrote is *not* what we believe."

As important as the 28 Fundamental Beliefs are, however, we must be careful to use them rightly. Doctrine cannot save us; only Jesus can. If we focus on the Fundamental Beliefs instead of on Jesus, we run the risk of falling into the same error as our pioneers who emphasized the Law and the Sabbath over the gospel. The young preachers Waggoner and Jones, backed up by Ellen White, were used by the Lord to bring us back on track.

The Acid Test

Let us hear again the word of the Lord:

"Having loved his own who were in the world, he now showed them the full extent of his love" (John 13:1, NIV 1984).

"A new command I give you: Love one another. As I have loved you, so you must love one another. By this everyone will know that you are my disciples, if you love one another" (John 13:34-35, NIV).

PART III

Coda

"Yes, I'm on my way! I'll be there soon!
I'm bringing my payroll with me.
I'll pay all people in full for their life's work.
I'm A to Z, the First and the Final, Beginning and Conclusion."
—Revelation 22:13, MSG

CHAPTER TEN

Two Women, Two Seats

December 1, 1955, a woman sitting at the rear of a bus in Birmingham, Alabama, was arrested and jailed. Her offense? She refused to give up her seat on the bus.

Rosa Parks was black; the passenger who wanted her seat was white.

By refusing to surrender her seat, Rosa Parks broke the prevailing Alabama law. More than 60 years later, few people would call her a lawbreaker who deserved to be punished. To most Americans, what she did was right. Rosa Parks has become an American hero.

Fast forward to the Seventh-day Adventist Church in 2018. Officers of union conferences who refuse to cease ordaining women ministers find themselves in a situation similar in basic respects to the one faced by Rosa Parks. For three Annual Councils in succession, General Conference leaders seem determined to punish "the non-compliant unions." They have failed twice, but they refuse to give up—while all around us people are desperate and dying for the hope that only Jesus brings. I marvel at this misdirection of time and resources.

If the latest proposal from General Conference leaders gains a majority vote, these union leaders will be stripped of voice and vote in the church's councils.

This would be a new day for the Seventh-day Adventist Church. From the earliest years of our existence, we have staunchly upheld individual conscience as something conferred by the Lord Himself. We have argued for religious freedom in countless courts. We have taken a public, official stand—not only on behalf of Adventists but also for others whose views we do not share but whose religious liberty is under threat.

All that will change if the action passes to "punish" union leaders for obeying their conscience. We will be found in the extraordinary position of "punishing" our own because they put conscience ahead of General Conference policy.

It will be a sad day for this church.

It must not happen.

I pray that it will not happen.

Let me share my thinking about this momentous situation. I do so as a voice—the voice of a layperson who resides in the Pacific Union, one of the unions that finds itself caught in the crosshairs. I will confine my remarks to this union—this part of the Adventist family where I attend church each Sabbath and return tithes and offerings.

Let me say it loud and clear: there is no "rebellion" in the Pacific Union.

To suggest otherwise is arrant nonsense. Life and ministry go forward quietly and powerfully for the glory of the Lord and His mission. Sick people are being helped and healed every day. Elementary schools, academies, colleges, and universities minister to children and young people. The word of God is proclaimed Sabbath by Sabbath by pastors, many of whom are women.

The Lord has blessed the Pacific Union. Here we find the church's premier Adventist institution—Loma Linda University and Medical Center. "Loma Linda" has become a name known throughout the world for the quality of its education, medical ministry, and research.

But Loma Linda University Health is not all one finds here, not by far. Adventist Health nonprofit health system serves more than 80 communities on the West Coast and Hawaii. Founded on Adventist heritage and values, Adventist Health provides care in hospitals, clinics, home care agencies, hospice agencies, and retirement centers in both rural and urban communities. These health professionals are transforming the American healthcare experience with a whole-person focus on physical, mental, spiritual, and social healing.

You will find this whole-person focus in the union's school system as well, recognizing that the student is more than just a mind to be filled with facts— preschool through university.

In this union one finds La Sierra University, a top-drawer institution with fine faculty and an outstanding campus. And Pacific Union College, an institution famous for its education for more than a century.

And more, much more: many hospitals and schools, agencies too many to list, dedicated to a large variety of ministries.

This is a wealthy and faithful union. Over the last four decades $4.88 billion in tithe has been carefully accounted for and distributed by the Pacific Union Conference to the properly assigned levels of the church, including the General Conference Treasury. That is *billions, not millions.*

Can any other union in global Adventism approach this figure? Does this sound like a union "in rebellion"? Nonsense!

But the picture could change, perhaps drastically, if the General Conference leaders persist in their punitive action and succeed in gaining a majority vote at the 2018 Annual Council.

Many, perhaps a large number of loyal Seventh-day Adventist members, will rise up and protest against what they perceive as a morally indefensible action. They will express their righteous anger in the most effective way they know—through their pocketbooks.

Inevitably, tithe returns to the General Conference Treasury will take a hit, perhaps a catastrophic hit. If this happens, it will not be because of rebellion. It will simply be because these Adventists followed the longstanding American principle of "no taxation without representation."

Respectfully, I offer my advice to the General Conference leaders: *Don't kill the goose that lays the golden egg.*

So I urge: Please, leave Pacific Union Conference alone to carry out its mission. Don't get in the way. Things are going well here. Don't, please don't mess it up.

I know personally the officers of the General Conference. They are good people, servants of the Lord who labor long and hard, seeking the best good for the Seventh-day Adventist Church. Somehow they have convinced themselves that the unity of the worldwide Seventh-day Adventist Church requires that the non-compliant unions be brought into line.

I can appreciate their passion for unity—I share it—but I think that the way they hope to achieve unity is dead wrong. Not only will it *not* preserve unity, it will have the opposite effect. Its result will be disunity: possible fracturing of the body and grievous harm to the mission with which the Lord has entrusted us.

What should General Conference leaders do in this situation? Nothing. Do nothing to upset what the Lord is doing through men and women in the Pacific Union. Let us alone to do our job. People and pastors are weary of being called disloyal and rebellious. We aren't.

To many of us here, the ordination of women pastors is a moral issue just as clearly as was Rosa Park's decision not to give up her seat on the bus. Don't trample on our conscience.

Wherein is ordination of women a moral issue? The answer is simple. You don't need a Ph.D. to understand it.

Church policy stipulates that administrative positions require ordination. But General Conference policy limits ordination to male members of the clergy, so women are excluded from conference administration. No matter how capable or qualified a woman may be, the church imposes a glass ceiling based on gender alone.

This is discrimination—no other word for it.

Logically and Theologically

Beyond the moral issue, the proposed disciplinary measure makes no sense logically or theologically.

The Adventist Church is organized into 13 divisions worldwide. In at least seven of these divisions women are serving in full-time ministry. Furthermore, in most of these seven divisions women, after they demonstrate their calling, are set apart by a special service called "commissioning."

But note: *The commissioning service is 100 percent identical to the service that sets apart male ministers. The only difference is that for males the service is called "ordination" but for females it is "commissioning."* Here lies the crux of the matter: The Bible, which we Adventists claim to take as our rule of faith and practice, makes no distinction between ordination and commissioning. Not a hair's difference.

Ordination simply means commissioning, nothing more.

The General Conference leaders have painted themselves into a logical and theological corner.

To make the point crystal clear: If the officers of the Pacific Union would just call the setting apart ceremony for women ministers "commissioning," the General Conference leaders would have no complaint against them, because policy permits women ministers to be "commissioned."

"Commissioned," but not "ordained."

Although on a biblical basis, the two terms are identical.

In light of these facts, charges of "rebellion" and "non-compliance" fall flat. The whole matter is one of words—words only.

Incredible: Adventists have been wasting time and resources for the last many years on a word game. When will we get real and focus on mission to dying, desperate men and women?

Well, you may reply, if ordination and commissioning are alternate names for one and the same service, why not simply use the non-loaded term "commissioning" instead of "ordination" for setting apart women pastors?

The answer is also simple: Because General Conference policy perpetuates the unbiblical distinction between ordination and commissioning. It restricts election to administrative leadership to those who are "ordained," as we already noted.

The way out of the mess in which we Adventists find ourselves is straightforward: *Either* drop the term "ordination" for everyone, both male and female, and call all pastors "commissioned" *or* drop the term "commissioning" for women pastors and substitute "ordination."

Are you wondering yet why there's all this fuss over something that boils down to arguments over words? I am.

And that's not all. One final point to chew over.

Although many unions in the world church employ women pastors, for whatever reasons the General Conference leaders seem to have focused on the two unions of the North American Division where women pastors are being ordained. *But what about China?*

In China Adventists have a large and growing work—and it is led by women pastors, many of whom have been ordained. In China the state oversees the operation of the seminaries that provide training for the ministry. Large numbers of Adventist women who feel called to the gospel ministry receive their training in these seminaries, *and on completion of the course of studies they are formally ordained.*

What am I saying? That in China the Adventist Church is thriving under the leadership of ordained women pastors.

How come the General Conference does not seek to bring these "non-compliant" women pastors into line?

I think the answer is obvious. They would risk shutting down our work in China. The dictates of mission demand that the women pastors not be hindered in their work.

Likewise, the dictates of mission in the Pacific Union demand that women pastors not be hamstrung in fulfilling their calling.

The Bubble

I worked at General Conference headquarters for some 25 years. I counted it a privilege; I still do.

But now, 11 years removed from that rarefied atmosphere, some thoughts trouble me. Has the General Conference fallen prey to the malaise that afflicts that other headquarters located in the Washington, DC, area: the United States Congress?

Men and women (mainly men) get elected to Congress. Probably most come to town hoping to make a difference for the good of the country. They gradually learn how things work: the levers of power, the machinery, the committees that are key to the system. They put in long hours, participate in endless debate.

And something slowly happens to them. Washington, DC, is a beautiful city, especially in the spring of the year. (The climate in July and August is a different story!) They become seduced by the corridors of power, by the prestige that their office brings.

Washington and its dynamics take over their thinking, their lives. When they retire or are voted out of office, many hang around, finding jobs as highly-paid lobbyists or consultants. Podunk seems far away, out of sight and out of mind.

They have exchanged Podunk for the Washington bubble.

What happened to the high-minded ideals that brought them to Washington? What happened to the independent ideas that once motivated them? Life in the bubble subtly leached away their ideals. They spent so much time listening to others who toed the party line that the bubble then turned into an echo chamber.

And here am I, 11 years removed from Washington, wondering on my bed in the wee hours if something similar happens to the men and women (mainly men) who work at the General Conference.

Did the General Conference become a bubble to me?

Did I subtly, gradually become part of an echo chamber?

I must confess it: the answer, painful as it is to admit, is Yes.

As I think of what this chapter has covered—the logical and theological morass into which I think General Conference leaders have sunk—how else to figure out their thinking unless to see it in terms of the bubble and the echo chamber?

Two Women, Two Seats

Years hence, a researcher studying the Seventh-day Adventist Church in North America during the early 21st century will discover something incomprehensible: *according to the official record of the church, the largest conference in the division had no conference president!*

The official record is maintained in the SDA Yearbook, which is compiled and published annually. It lists every church entity, every conference, every president, every employee of the church worldwide. That is where you go to get the facts, the basic facts about the church. It is, as you might expect, a thick volume.

Now, go to the Yearbook for 2017 and look up the data for the Southeastern California Conference. You find members, names, institutions. But look for the name of the conference president, and what do you find? You find a blank.

According to the Yearbook, the church's official and authoritative record, the Southeastern California Conference has no president. Nor did it have (according to the Yearbook) in 2016 or 2015.

But Southeastern California does have a president. The conference is growing, financially sound, and ably led.

Its president, Dr. Roberts, was elected by a large majority of members at a duly called constituency meeting.

What then must one say about the Yearbook?

That it is misleading?

That it is inaccurate?

That it lies?

This seemingly incomprehensible fact has a simple but ever-so-revealing explanation: Dr. Roberts is Dr. Sandra Roberts—yes, a woman!

When the office of conference president became vacant several years ago, delegates at the duly appointed constituency meeting selected the person whom they considered best qualified for the job—conference secretary Dr. Sandra Roberts.

General Conference policy stipulates that in order to serve as a conference president, one must have been ordained. Dr. Roberts has been ordained, but the General Conference leaders refuse to acknowledge it. And her name is not included in the official record.

What about this General Conference decision? What to call it?

Petty?

Vindictive?

Outrageous?

Discriminatory?

You decide.

Thus the long, sad story of Adventist women in ministry can be boiled down to something anyone can readily grasp: two women, two seats.

The first woman was Rosa Parks. She was arrested and jailed because she was deemed in violation of the law of the State of Alabama.

Rosa Parks was denied a seat on the bus because she was black.

The second woman is Sandra Roberts. She was elected by the people of the Adventist Church in the Southeastern California Conference. When she goes to Adventist Church headquarters for the meeting of the Annual Council, she isn't recognized along with the other conference presidents. Sandra Roberts is denied a seat at the table because she is a woman.

Noelene and I now live in retirement in the Southeastern California Conference. We return our tithes each month through the conference office.

As tithe-paying, loyal members of the Seventh-day Adventist Church, we protest this basic injustice, this discriminatory treatment of our conference president.

This denial of basic morality is a case of policy run amok, policy being employed against ethics.

It is a denial of authentic Adventism.

For a while we wondered why the members of the largest conference in America don't rise up and demand that the blatant injustice be corrected at once.

At last we figured out why: *for a great many good, loyal, lifelong Adventists the actions of the General Conference no longer mean much to them. Whatever General Conference leaders may vote or not vote doesn't make a straw of difference.*

The General Conference has become irrelevant to them.

For us that has been an exceedingly sad discovery. With it has come a couple of other facts that I hope and pray leaders in Silver Spring will take to heart:

First, the General Conference needs the Pacific Union more than the Pacific Union needs the General Conference. If the General Conference by some circumstance should just go away, the Seventh-day Adventist Church in the Pacific Union would continue, albeit with loss. If, however, the Pacific Union were to disappear, the impact on the General Conference would be catastrophic.

Second, the church is a *volunteer* body. There should be no coercion, no compulsion in the church. We are Protestants! Our heritage goes back to the Reformers like Martin Luther. We have declared this movement to be heir to that great reform movement. In this context, talk of "punishment" is totally out of place. It does not belong in the Adventist vocabulary; it is repugnant.

I write these thoughts in love, not anger; in sorrow, not in bitterness. I am not so naïve as to think my words will be welcomed in some quarters. Be that as it may, my boss is the Lord, the One who gave His life for me. More than anything else, I seek to do what is right in His eyes.

In recent years I have been in conversation with an individual, now retired, whom I love and hold in the highest esteem. This brother, who is known to most readers of this book, throughout a long ministry is acclaimed for unswerving integrity, for courage, for speaking out when the times called for speaking out. This man once came within a handful of votes of being elected to lead the world Seventh-day Adventist Church.

This leader, like me, is deeply disturbed over current trends in the church, and in particular over the apparent fixation of General Conference leaders on "punishing" the so-called non-compliant unions. During one telephone exchange, he posed a question to me—a question that still rings in my ears.

"Brother Bill, please explain one matter to me. How come the officers of the General Conference, those who are aware of what is happening, don't speak out? Knowing what they know, how can they remain silent?"

How, indeed?

The Last Word

As important as the deliberations of the Annual Council undoubtedly are, this book must not end there. Jesus must be the Last Word.

Jesus is the Alpha. He was, before all else. He was in the beginning. He was the Beginning. He was/is the Word, without beginning, without end.

"And the Word became flesh and lived among us, and we have seen his glory, the glory as of a father's only son, full of grace and truth (John 1:14, NRSV).

He came from heaven to earth, trailing streams of light. We call Him Jesus.

We are all like jet planes flying through the expanse of the heavens, leaving ribbons of white against the blue. Our jet trails—no matter how bright—blur, fade, and disappear, melting into the expanse as though we'd never been.

But His never fades. So long as the sky shall endure, as long as men and women have eyes to see, the divine imprint left by Jesus will blossom and glow. The centuries as they roll cannot dim it; the scoffing of critics cannot expunge it; the base neglect of those too blind to recognize it cannot annul it.

Against that trail of light we measure every other life. Our riches or fame, our learning or degrees, our accomplishments or our status: these things do not count anymore—only the extent to which our little day in the noonday sun has in some small measure left a trail like His.

One day jets and jet trails will be no more. But Jesus will be, be All.

He is the Omega.

He is the Last Word.

And that word is love.

Made in United States
Orlando, FL
30 March 2022

16307337R00102